Handbook of Indexing Techniques

A Guide for Beginning Indexers

Second Edition

Linda K. Fetters

with contributions from

Cynthia D. Bertelsen
and
Do Mi Stauber

FimCo Books

Published by FimCo Books
4531 Ayers St. #220
Corpus Christi, TX 78415
e-mail: lfetters@caller.infi.net

Table of Contents

Preface

Introduction

This handbook on indexing techniques is intended for three groups of people:

♦ occasional indexers, such as authors and technical writers, who may be called upon to index their own books;

♦ anyone interested in becoming a professional indexer who is looking for concrete examples or techniques for learning how to index;

♦ librarians who need a review of indexing techniques.

In this book you will find explanations of indexing techniques along with examples of each topic discussed. Since it is not an exhaustive study of indexing, the bibliographies at the end of most chapters contain many suggestions for further reading and study.

In addition to complete updates of information in the first edition and its revisions, this second edition of the *Handbook* contains five new chapters, including a reprint of Do Mi Stauber's article, "Jewels in the Cavern," and four by Cynthia D. Bertelsen on reference works for indexers.

Acknowledgments

I would like to thank Linda Webster, who edited early versions of the book and contributed many examples; Frances Lennie, who encouraged me to complete and publish this book, and who also contributed examples; Elsie Lynn, who proofread the original manuscript and offered suggestions; and Hudson Fetters, for his constant support.

Chapter I
Learning to Index

Many people are interested in becoming indexers at this particular time. Some have experience in the publishing field, some are women who want to work at home on a part-time basis while they also care for their children. Others want to join the working-at-home revolution set in motion by the availability of personal computers with communication links. Professional indexers and members of the American Society of Indexers (ASI) receive numerous phone calls from people asking how to get started. Before thinking about the business aspects of self-employment, prospective indexers should first consider how to learn their intended craft.

If you are reading this book because you have to write an index right away, skip this chapter and go on to chapter 2.

Formal Courses and Seminars

Some schools of library and information science offer courses in indexing and abstracting. Your public library has one or more reference books that list these schools. You may contact the school nearest you for requirements. Library schools sometimes offer one-day seminars in indexing. Extension programs at some universities include courses in indexing that are open to people who are not enrolled in regular courses at the university.

Private companies also offer occasional indexing seminars. For example, EEl Communications (66 Canal Center Plaza, Suite 200, Alexandria, VA 22314–1538, 703–683–0683, http://www.eeicom.com) presents a seminar on basic indexing. You may be able to find such seminars in your area by checking the yellow pages under editorial services.

The American Society of Indexers (ASI) Web page keeps an up-to-date list of conferences, workshops, and seminars related to indexing. In addition, ASI publishes a directory of courses and workshops, entitled *Directory of Indexing and Abstracting Courses and Seminars*. You can find more information about ASI and other indexing societies under "Professional Organizations" on page 7.

Correspondence Courses

The U.S. Department of Agriculture offers two correspondence courses: Basic Indexing and Applied Indexing. These courses are prepared and graded by experienced ASI members. They provide much needed feedback on your progress in learning to index. For a free catalog, call 202-720-7123, or write to Correspondence Study Program, Graduate School, USDA, Room 1112, South Agriculture Building, 14th and Independence Ave. S.W., Washington, DC 20250-9911. The e-mail address is correspond@grad.usda.gov, and the Web site URL is http://grad.usda.gov/corres/corpro.html.

Another correspondence course, the Book Indexing Postal Tutorials (BIPT) is offered by Ann Hall of Scotland. "BIPT consists of five tutorials, involving the compilation of indexes to short texts, chosen to represent most of the problems an indexer is likely to meet. A sixth optional tutorial involves the creation of an index to a complete book. It is a practical course, with personal one4o-one tuition and detailed individual marking." The first tutorial and booklets cost £45 (£50 overseas). If you continue past the first tutorial, the remaining four tutorials cost £125 (£145 overseas). The optional sixth tutorial costs £45 (£50 overseas).

For further details send a self-addressed, stamped envelope to Ann Hall, The Lodge, Sidmount Avenue, Moffat DG1O 9B5, Scotland. Call or fax 01683 220440, or e-mail 101233.2664@compuserve.com.

Self-Training

In the first edition of the ASI publication, *Starting an Indexing Business,* new indexers reported that they learned how to index by taking courses (as noted above), and by several other methods. A few reported apprenticing themselves to experienced indexers (be aware, however, that many indexers are too busy keeping up with their work schedules to have time to take on apprentices). Others learned on their own by finding and studying indexing textbooks, publishers' style guides, and indexing standards. These resources are described later in this chapter.

Society of Indexers Training Manuals

A series of self-training manuals has been published by The Society of Indexers (SI) in Great Britain, as follows:

Arrangement and Presentation of Indexes by Pat F. Booth, 2nd ed., 1991. Topics include alphabetical and nonalphabetical arrangement of indexes, word-by-word and letter-by-letter arrangements, an overview of book and journal publishing, layout of index entries, and the presentation of copy for reproduction.

Choice and Form of Entries by Pat F. Booth and Mary Piggott, 2nd ed., revised by Pat F. Booth, 1995. This manual discusses indexable elements of content, specificity and exhaustivity, form of headings and subheadings, when to use singular or plural nouns, arrangement of entries, types of cross-references, how to handle proper names, and many other areas of concern.

Documents, Authors, Users, Indexers by Pat F. Booth, 2nd ed., 1990. Briefly defines the functions and characteristics of indexes, presents a glossary of indexing terminology, and describes various types of documents and types of indexes.

Information Sources and Reference Tools by K. G. B. Bakewell. 2nd ed. revised by Pat F. Booth, 1993. Bakewell's original article appeared as "Reference Books for Indexers" in *The Indexer* 15, no 3 (1987): 131–140. The revised manual includes information on standards, textbooks and periodicals for indexers. It also outlines the use and construction of thesauri, and describes the use of libraries, databases, and reference sources.

The Business of Indexing by Pat F. Booth and Elizabeth Wallis, 1989. Describes the basics of running an indexing business.

A more complete description of these manuals appears on the Society of Indexers' Web site and also in most issues of The Indexer, which also includes prices and ordering information. To purchase the course, contact Wendy Burrow at the Society of Indexers (SI) Administrative Office. Contact information for SI can be found under "Professional Organizations" on page 7.

Internet Discussion Groups

Although not strictly a method for learning how to index, discussion groups (mailing lists) can be very helpful for beginning indexers. ASI's Web site lists current indexing discussion groups, as well as many more related groups. The two e-mail lists of most relevance to new indexers are INDEX-L and Indexstudents.

INDEX-L

INDEX-L has about 800 members, mostly from the English-speaking indexing communities, but not all members participate in the day-to-day discussion. Many are "lurkers" who are content to follow the "threads" of the discussion, or participate occasionally. Anyone can pose a question related to indexing. List members never seem to tire of answering the same questions, so new members should not be afraid to ask for advice and assistance. To subscribe to INDEX-L, send an e-mail message to listserv@bingvmb.cc.binghamton.edu as follows:

> SUBSCRIBE INDEX-L *firstname lastname*

substituting your own first and last names. No other information should appear in the message, and you should disable the automatic signature option of your e-mail program, if you use one. To unsubscribe, send a message to the same address as follows:

> SIGNOFF INDEX-L

You can also read or get copies of previous discussions (archives), as outlined on the ASI Web site.

Indexstudents

According to the ASI Web site, "Indexstudents is for all persons interested in discussing issues related to learning to index books, magazines, databases, and the World Wide Web. Primary, discussion will focus on the experiences and questions of individuals taking the USDA Graduate School courses." For more information and to subscribe, contact: http://www.onelist.com/subscribe.cgi/indexstudents.

WINDMAIL

The goal of The Web Indexers' Mailing list is to provide a forum for the discussion of Web Indexing, including "traditional-style" indexes, "micro" indexing of a single Web page, "midi" indexing of multiple pages, "Web-wide" indexing for providing centralized access to widely scattered material which falls under a single heading (e.g., every Web page dealing authoritatively with breast cancer)," and "macro" schemes designed to simply or unify access to large numbers of Web pages falling under many different headings (e.g., every Web page dealing authoritatively with any medical topic). For more information or to subscribe, go to the Australian Society of Indexers' Web site at http://www.zeta.org.au/~aussi/webindexing/webindexmlist.htm. Web indexing is discussed more fully in chapter 7.

Writing Practice Indexes

The best way to learn indexing is to index. If you don't have any means of getting feedback on your indexing efforts, find a book you like and create your own index for it. Compare your index to the one in the book. Remember that two people seldom index anything the same way. Studies have found very little consistency between terms chosen by different indexers for the same document.* You can learn a great deal, nevertheless, by comparing your indexing style with that of other indexers.

Studying the indexes of award-winning indexers is another method for learning how to index. These indexers received the ASI/Wilson Award for their outstanding work:

1979—Hans Wellisch, author and indexer, and John Wiley, publisher: *The Conversion of Scripts: Its Nature, History and Utilization.*

1980—Linda I. Solow, indexer, and MIT Press, publisher: *Beyond Orpheus: Studies in Musical Structures*, by David Epstein.

1981—Delight Ansley, indexer, and Random House, publisher: *Cosmos*, by Carl Sagan.

1982—Catherine Fix, indexer, and Saunders Company, publisher: *Diagnosis of Bone and Joint Disorders* by Resnick and Niwayama.

1983—No award given.

1984—Trish Yancey, indexer, and Information Handling Service, publisher: *Index and Directory of the U.S. Industry Standards.*

---

* Karen Markey, "Interindexer Consistency Tests: A Literature Review...." *Library and Information Science Research* 6, no. 2 (1984): 155–177.

1985—Sidney W. Cohen, indexer, and Random House, publisher: *The Experts Speak,* by Cerf and Navasky.

1986—Marjorie Hyslop, indexer, and American Society of Metals, publisher: *Metals Handbook.*

1987—No award given.

1988—Jeanne Moody, indexer, and Institute for Wildlife Research, publisher: *Raptor Management Techniques Manual*, by Beth A. Giron Pendleton.

1989—Philip James, indexer, and Butterworth, publisher: *Medicine for the Practicing Physician,* 2d ed., edited by J. Willis Hurst.

1990—Marcia Carlson, indexer and Cornell University Press, publisher: *Nuclear Arms and Arms Control Debates,* by Lynn Eden and Steven Miller.

1991—Nancy L. Daniels, indexer, and Van Nostrand Reinhold, publisher: *Beyond Public Architecture: Strategies for Design Evaluation*, by Hamid Shirvani.

1992—Rachel Jo Johnson, indexer, and Matthew Bender, publisher: *The American Law of Real Property*, by Arthur Gaudio.

1993—No award given.

1994—Patricia Deminna, indexer, and University of California Press, publisher: *Carnal Israel: Reading Sex in Talmudic Culture*, by Daniel Boyarin.

1995—Martin L. White, indexer, and University of Chicago Press, publisher: *The Promise of Pragmatism: Modernism and the Crisis of Knowledge and Authority*, by John Patrick Diggins.

1996—No award given.

1997—Gillian Northcott and Ruth Levitt, indexers, and Grove/Macmillan, publishers: *Grove Dictionary of Art*, edited by Joan Shoaf Turner.

1998—Laura Moss Gottlieb, indexer, and University of Wisconsin Press, publisher: *Dead Wrong*, by Michael A. Mello.

You may be interested in reading about some of the award winners and what they have to say about indexing. Articles from *The American Society of Indexers Newsletter/Key Words* can be found under "ASI/Wilson Award Winners" in the "Further Study" section at the end of the chapter.

Another way to get some practice is to volunteer to write an index for an institution or organization in your area. Most libraries have projects languishing in boxes for lack of staff. Many corporations have minutes or reports of board meetings or research reports for which they would love to have an index. Once you complete such a project, you have a published index to list on your resume'.

Every freelance indexer in business now has faced the same hurdle: learning to index and finding the first job. Studying, determination, hard work, and luck boosted them along the road to self-employment as indexers. Several articles in *Key Words* and two ASI booklets address this topic. They are listed in the "Finding Clients" section of the bibliography on page 12.

Professional Organizations

Since indexers are generally few and far between, you can find a great deal of support by joining an indexing society. Here is a list of names and addresses for English-speaking indexers:

> American Society of Indexers
> P.O. Box 39366
> Phoenix, AZ 85069-9366
> Phone: 602-979-5514
> Fax: 602-530-4088
> e-mail: info@ASIndexing.org
> http:/www.ASIndexing.org

> Australian Society of Indexers (AusSI)
> G.P.O. Box 1251L, Melbourne
> Victoria 3001, Australia
> Fax: 03-670-0138
> e-mail: aussi@zeta.org
> http://www.zeta.org.au/~aussi/

Indexing and Abstracting Society of Canada/
Societé Canadienne pour l'analyse de documents (IASC/SCAD)
P.O. Box 744
Station F
Toronto, Ontario, Canada M4Y 2N6
http://www.tornade.ere.umontreal.ca/-turner/iasc/home.html

Society of Indexers (SI)
Globe Centre
Penistone Road
Sheffield S6 3AE
England
Phone: +44 (0)114 281 3060
Fax: +44 (0)114 281 3061
e-mail: admin@socind.demon.co.uk
http://www.socind.demon.co.uk

Membership in the American Society of Indexers (ASI) includes subscriptions to *Key Words,* the newsletter of the American Society of Indexers, as well as *The Indexer,* journal of the Society of Indexers and the affiliated American, Australian, and Canadian societies. ASI sponsors one annual conference per year; local chapters hold one or more meetings per year. Chapters and their activities appear in the "Networking Notebook" section in each issue of *Key Words,* as well as ASI's Web site. Contact information and URLs for chapter Web pages are included.

The ASI publishes a variety of books about indexing through its agent:

Information Today, Inc.
143 Old Marlton Pike
Medford, NJ 08055
1-800-300-9868
e-mail: custserv@infotoday.com
http://www.infotoday.com

Standards and Index Evaluation

Indexing preparation standards are available from several organizations, whose contact information appears below. The international standard can be obtained from the International Organization for Standardization (ISO): *Information and Documentation Guidelines for the Content, Organization and Pres-*

entation of Indexes (ISO 999:1996). It is very expensive, however, so you might want to check with your local library for a copy. Two articles in *The Indexer* summarize and discuss the practical use of ISO 999 and other standards. See Booth (1997) and Calvert (1996) in the "Standards" section of the bibliography on page 12.

The British Standards Institution (BSI) publishes several standards relevant to indexing: BS 6529:1984, *Recommendations for Examining Documents, Determining Their Subjects and Selecting Indexing Terms;* and BS 1749:1985, *Recommendations for Alphabetical Arrangement and the Filing Order of Numbers and Symbols.*

The National Information Standards Organization (NISO) sells several books of interest to indexers, including *Guidelines for Indexes and Related Information Retrieval Devices, Challenges in Indexing Electronic Text and Images,* and *A Guide to Alphanumeric Arrangement and Sorting,* among others.

Standards Contact Information

The International Organization for Standardization
1 rue de Varembé
Case Postale 56
CH-1211 Genève 20
Switzerland
e-mail: central@iso.ch
http://www.iso.ch

British Standards Institution
389 Chiswick High Road
London W4 4AL
United Kingdom
e-mail: info@bsi.org.uk
http://www.bsi.org.uk
Phone: +44 (0)181 996 9000
Fax: +44 (0) 181 996 7400

National Information Standards Organization
4733 Bethesda Ave., Suite 300
Bethesda, MD 20814
301-654-2512
e-mail: nisohq@niso.org
http://www.niso.org

Other Guidelines

One objective of the American Society of Indexers (as well as the other indexing societies) is "to improve the quality of indexing and to promote standards for those who compile or edit indexes and abstracts." One of the ways ASI promotes standards is by offering, in conjunction with the H. W. Wilson Company, the ASI/Wilson Award for "excellence in indexing of an English language monograph or other nonserial publication published in the United States during the previous calendar year." The criteria are reproduced on the next few pages, with permission from ASI. The criteria, as well as the mechanics of the award process, are published on ASI's Web site. (See the "Index Evaluation" section of the bibliography on page 12 for articles on index evaluation.)

Criteria for the ASI/Wilson Award

The criteria for the American Society of Indexers/H. W. Wilson Company Award are guided by the standards established by the American National Standards Institute (ANSI).

Introductory Note

An introductory note should be present if any aspect of the index requires explanation. It should be clear and well expressed, and it should establish the basis of selection and omission of indexable matter.

Physical Format, Typography and Style

The index entries should be presented in a format, typography, and style that provides maximum ease of scanning the index and locating individual entries. A clear and logical organization should be evident. Spacing, indentations, and general page design should present a page that is aesthetically pleasing.

The index should be appropriate in size to the number of pages in the publication and the type of material contained therein.

Content of the Index

The index must bring together references to similar concepts that are scattered in the text, or that are expressed in varying terminology. This can be done through the establishment of a single heading and a set of subheadings, through the use of cross-references, or through other appropriate devices.

All significant items in the text must appear in the index. However, if there is a category of material that is not indexed, this should be stated in the introduction.

Items and concepts in the text must be represented in the index by appropriate, precise, accurate, unambiguous headings.

The index entry headings should be consistent in form and in usage. Inclusion of synonymous headings and spelling variations, if used, should be intentional to facilitate access.

The index should represent the text and not be a vehicle for expressing the indexer's own views and interests.

Structure and Accuracy of the Index Entries

The index entries should be arranged in a recognizable, or stated searchable order, such as alphabetical, classified, chronological, or numerical order.

The locators given in the index should tally with the text.

Strings of undifferentiated locators should generally be avoided by use of appropriate subheadings or other appropriate devices. If the number of locators in a given entry is so large that aspects of the heading are not adequately differentiated, additional headings, subheadings, or modifiers should be introduced. Headings should be as specific as the nature of the collection permits, and the purposes of the users require.

There must be a sufficient number of cross-references in the index so that related items are connected, and obsolete or idiosyncratic terms in the text are related to terms in current use.

Abbreviations, acronyms, symbols, or other abridgment of a word or phrase should be explained in an appropriate manner.

Further Study

ASI/Wilson Award Winners

Cohen, Sydney: "Profile of the 1984 Wilson Award Winner." *American Society of Indexers Newsletter* no. 72 (1985): 16–17.

Daniels, Nancy L. "Daniels Wins ASI/Wilson Award." *American Society of Indexers Newsletter* no. 105 (1991): 21.

Deminna, Patrica. "The Award-Winning Index for 1994." *Key Words* 2, no. 3 (1994): 1

Fields, Mary: "ASI Profiles." *American Society of Indexers Newsletter* no. 67 (1984): 15.

Gottlieb, Laura Moss: "Wilson Award Acceptance Speech." *Key Words* 6, no. 4 (1998): 15–17.

Hyslop, Marjorie Rud: "Marjorie Hyslop Wins H.W. Wilson Indexing Award." *American Society of Indexers Newsletter* no. 77 (1986): 11.

Johnson, Rachel Jo: "Jo Johnson Wins Wilson Award." *American Society of Indexers Newsletter* no. 110 (1992): 1, 22.

Northcott, Gillian and Ruth Levitt: "The Wilson Award for Excellence in Indexing, 1997." *Key Words* 5, nos. 3-4 (1997): 1, 14–15.

White, Martin L.: "The 1995 ASI/Wilson Award Winner." *Key Words* 3, no. 3 (1995): 1, 42–45.

Education

Corbett, MaryAnn. *Directory of Indexing and Abstracting Courses and Seminars.* Medford, NJ: American Society of Indexers, 1998.

Hall, Ann. "Problems, Some Usual (Marking Book Indexing Postal Tutorials)." *Indexer* 20, no. 4 (1997): 182–184.

Manley, Shirley and Harwood, Norma. "Bringing It Home: Learning to Index Books by Correspondence." *Indexer* 20, no. 4 (1997): 185–187.

Finding Clients

Cohen, Barbara E. "Luck is Hard Work." *Key Words* 1, no.5 (1993): 10–13.

Leach, Anne, *Marketing Your Indexing Services.* 2d ed. Medford, NJ: American Society of Indexers, 1998.

Spence, Matthew. "How to Get Clients." *Key Words* 1, no. 4 (1993): 4–7, 21.

Wyman, Pilar. "The Business of Being in Business." *Key Words* 6, no. 2 (1998): 14–20.

Zafran, Enid. *Starting an Indexing Business.* 3rd ed. Medford, NJ: American Society of Indexers, 1998.

Index Evaluation

Billick, David. "Reviewing the Wilson Award Submissions." *American Society of Indexers Newsletter* no.104 (1991): 4–5.

Fetters, Linda. "The Wilson Award for 1992." *Key Words* 1, no.6 (1993): 1, 5.

McGovern, Carolyn. "How to Evaluate Indexes." *Key Words* 1, no. 9 (1993): 1, 21.

Standards

Anderson, James D.. *Guidelines for Indexes and Related Information Retrieval Devices.* Oxon Hill, MD: NISO, 1997.

Booth, Pat F. "Good Practice in Indexing—The New Edition of International Standard ISO 999." Indexer 20, no.3 (1997): 114.

British Standards Institution. *Recommendations for Alphabetical Arrangement and the Filing Order of Numbers and Symbols.* London: BSI, 1985.

British Standards Institution. *Recommendations for Examining Documents, Determining Their Subjects, and Selecting Indexing Terms.* London: BSI, 1984.

Calvert, Drusilla. "Deconstructing Indexing Standards." Indexer 20, no. 2 (1996): 74–78.

Milstead, Jessica. "Indexing Standards." In *Indexing Tradition and Innovation: Proceedings of the 22nd Annual Conference of the American Society of Indexers.* Port Aransas, TX: American Society of Indexers, 1991.

Wellisch, Hans H. *A Guide to Alphanumeric Arrangement and Sorting.* Oxon Hill, MD: NISO, 1999.

National Information Standards Organization. *Guidelines for the Construction, Format, and Management of Monolingual Thesauri.* Oxon Hill, MD: NISO, 1993.

Textbooks

Borko, Harold and Charles L. Bernier. *Indexing Concepts and Methods.* New York: Academic Press, 1978.

Cleveland, Donald B. and Ana D. Cleveland. *Introduction to Indexing and Abstracting.* 2d ed. Englewood, CO: Libraries Unlimited, 1990.

Collison, Robert L. *Indexes and Indexing: Guide to the Indexing of Books, Periodicals, Music, Recordings, Films, and Other Material....* London: Benn, 1972.

Knight, G. Norman. *Indexing, The Art of: A Guide to the Indexing of Books and Periodicals.* London: Allen & Unwin, 1979.

Lancaster, F. W. *Indexing & Abstracting in Theory & Practice.* Champaign, IL: Graduate School of Library and Information Science, 1991.

Mulvany, Nancy. *Indexing Books.* Chicago: University of Chicago Press, 1994.

Thatcher, Virginia S. *Indexes: Writing, Editing, Production.* Lanham, MD: Scarecrow Press, 1995.

Wellisch, Hans H. *Indexing from A to Z.* 2d ed. New York: Wilson Company, 1995.

Bibliographies on Indexing

Wellisch, Hans H. *Indexing and Abstracting: An International Bibliography.* Santa Barbara, CA: ABC-Clio, 1980.

Wellisch, Hans H. *Indexing and Abstracting 1977–1981: An International Bibliography.* Santa Barbara, CA: ABC-Clio, 1984.

Wellisch, Hans H. "Indexing and Abstracting: A Current-Awareness Bibliography." Parts 1–8, *Indexer* 15, no.1 (1986): 29–36; 15, no.2 (1986): 95–98; 15, no.3 (1987): 159–162; 15, no.4 (1987): 219–229; 16, no.1 (1988): 33–39; 16, no.2 (1988): 107–110; 16, no. 3 (1989): 181–188; 16, no.4 (1989): 255–260.

Wheeler, Jean. "Indexing: A Current-Awareness Bibliography." Parts 1–9, *In-dexer* 18, no.3 (1993): 173–186; 18, no.4 (1993): 247–258; 19, no.1 (1994): 37A4; 18, no.3 (1995): 193–200; 20 no.1 (1996): 25–30; 20, no.3 (1997): 137–140; 20, no. 4 (1997): 201–207; 21 no. 1 (1998): 25–28.

Wheeler, Jean. "Indexing: A Current-Awareness Bibliography: Index to Parts 1–9." *Indexer* 19, no. 2 (1994): 111–122; 20, no. 2 (1996): 81–86; 21, no. 2 (1998): 77–84.

Chapter 2
Starting the Index

Whether you create an index on a personal computer or on 3 x 5 cards, you use the same basic techniques and principles. Although this chapter refers almost exclusively to book indexing, these techniques and principles can be applied to technical manuals, magazines, in-house databases, or various kinds of subject files (vertical files, personal collections of articles, and office files).

What is an Index?

An index is a tool for locating specific information contained within a document. Readers can get a good overview of what a document contains by reading the table of contents, but they cannot find the exact page on which a particular bit of information appears. A good index quickly guides readers to any significant piece of information.

A common mistake made by first-time or occasional indexers is giving too much information in the index entries. An index is not a summary of the book's content or an extended capsule discussion of the major subjects treated in the book. If index entries are specific and concise, the index will be an effective finding tool—its primary purpose.

How readers use an index depends on their particular information needs. Students researching a topic for a term paper might start their search by looking under broad headings to become familiar with the subject, for example, world hunger. Researchers working in the field would go directly to specific information, such as the most recent statistics on food production in West Africa, or they may want to find out who is currently involved in nutrition projects in Central America. Indexes need to accommodate the needs of different types of readers, whether they are the general public, students, researchers, or scholars.

What the Index Includes

Indexes for books and magazines include names of important people, events, dates, and broad concepts. Indexes for scientific material may include chemical formulas, technical processes, and symbols. An index for a computer manual includes mostly processes, commands, and reports. Many times the material needs only a subject index. Other types of documents require author and title indexes. These are often separate indexes. Subject indexes are made up of main headings, subheadings that further distinguish different aspects of the main headings, and page references (or other types of locators) that refer to the location in the text where the information can be found.

A cookbook, for example, needs entries for the main ingredient of each recipe. In addition, it might include large headings for the various food groups such as breads, rice, vegetables, and meat. Depending on the type of cookbook, it might have entries for categories of foods like desserts, appetizers, main courses, and salads. Other topics could include the country of origin and recipe names. The worst cookbook indexes contain *only* recipe names!

The index usually excludes prefaces and acknowledgments (front matter). Appendixes may or may not be included. If an appendix contains a significant discussion of a topic, by all means include it. Often, appendix materials can be indexed lightly, indicating main ideas, without as much detail as for the text. For example, if a history of Central America included the text of the Monroe Doctrine in the appendix, you would index that item under Monroe Doctrine, but you would not index the specific details of the document.

Words that are listed in a glossary are not included in the index since a glossary, like an index, is a reference device. If the author discusses or defines a term in the book that also appears in the glossary, then the term should appear in the index, but do not include the glossary page reference for it. If there is any question about whether or not to include glossary terms, consult the editor for a determination.

In scholarly works, footnotes are indexed if they contain substantive information or further discussion of information found in the chapter. Do not index footnotes that are only bibliographical citations. Examples of footnotes appear in chapter 5.

Charts, tables, maps, photographs, or other illustrations should be included in the index. Some publishers designate illustrative materials with special typography, such as boldfaced page numbers for tables or italicized page numbers for figures. Often, "t" is appended to the page reference to designate tables, "f" for figures, and "(illus.)" for illustrations. The publisher should inform you of the preferred conventions. Any symbols or use of special typography should be explained in an introduction to the index. You may also designate illustrations as subheadings, as in the next example:

Central America
    map, 218

function keys
    quick reference chart, 2–7

Viewpoint

In planning an index, you have to think about who the audience will be and how they are going to look for information. It's important to respect the author's choice of terminology and the author's approach to the subject matter. The best indexes, however, are those that consider the readers' viewpoint as well as the author's terminology, since readers may not be familiar with the terms that are used in the text. Cross-references (described in chapter 5) can help readers get to the proper index heading.

For example, a veterinary medicine textbook uses the terms felines and canines rather than cats and dogs. The index should use the words *felines* and *canines* as the headings. The index should also include the following cross-references to help readers find the proper headings:

cats. *See* felines

dogs. *See* canines

A book for pet lovers on the care of dogs, cats, and other small animals, on the other hand, should use the term *dogs* as the main heading with a See reference as follows:

canines. *See* dogs

felines. *See* cats

Getting an Overview

Before you begin choosing words or phrases for the index (entries or headings), it is helpful to get an overview of the book. Start with the table of contents and introduction. Look at the conclusion. If each chapter contains an abstract or summary, pay particular attention to this information. Then skim the entire book, looking for chapter titles, subtitles, headers, and boldfaced or italicized text. Once you have a good idea of the content of the book, you are ready to choose subject headings.

If you feel unfamiliar with the topic or type of book you are indexing, you may find it helpful to go to a local library to look at indexes for similar types of books. Sometimes you might find a previous edition of the book you are indexing that you can use as a starting point.

Length of the Index

When you start to prepare the entries for a book index, you may wonder how many terms to choose from each page, or how long the index should be. There is no easy guide to follow. The more technical or scholarly the book, the more index entries per page. For example, one page may contain a short description of five authors and their literary works so you would have five or more entries for that page. Another page may contain a lengthy discussion of the work of one author, so there might be only one entry for that page. The text itself ultimately determines the density of the index.

Sometimes an editor will tell you how many pages or how many lines have been allotted for an index, which, to a large extent, will govern how detailed the index may be. If you must index under space constraints, proceed as if there were no space problems. When you have finished the index, you can combine subheadings or otherwise condense the index. It is better for the indexer to make those kinds of decisions rather than the editor.

Armed with the basic structure for starting your index, you are ready to start writing index entries. Chapter 3 describes techniques for choosing and phrasing headings and subheadings.

Further Study

Brogan, Hugh. "The Agony and the Ecstasy of a DIY Author-Indexer." *Indexer* 14, no. 3 (1985): 175–176.
Chicago Manual of Style. 14th ed. Chicago: University of Chicago Press, 1993.
Lancaster, F. W. *Indexing & Abstracting in Theory & Practice*. Champaign, IL: Graduate School of Library and Information Science, 1991.
Mulvany, Nancy. *Indexing Books*. Chicago: University of Chicago Press, 1994.
Ridehalgh, Nan. "The Design of Indexes." *Indexer* 14, no.3 (1985): 165–174.
Wellisch, Hans H. *Indexing from A to Z*. 2d ed. New York: Wilson Company, 1995.

Chapter 3
Writing the Index

Writing an index consists of reading the manuscript, marking names and concepts for inclusion, dividing complex topics into subheadings, and phrasing or editing the headings and subheadings.

Choosing and Writing Headings

For discussion purposes, assume that you will use the traditional indexing method, that is, marking index entries on a printed copy of the book, and writing or typing the index entries on 3 x 5 cards. Other techniques for recording index entries are summarized starting on page 31.

When you skimmed the chapters in the overview process, as described in chapter 2, you began to form the structure of the index. The next step is to read each chapter in detail, mark important text, and commit the index entries to paper or computer records. You will continue to build and modify the index structure as you work your way through the book.

Some indexers read the entire book before beginning to make entries. Although this may work for small books, it is not possible in all cases. Indexers sometimes receive books in installments—a few chapters per week—with a rush of chapters as the typesetting is completed. If you wait until you have all the pages before you begin to read and mark, you will not have enough time to complete the index by the deadline.

A good approach is to read and mark one chapter at a time and record the entries, either on 3 x 5 cards or as computer records in indexing software. This will allow you to keep track of the index structure and to modify that structure as you work your way through the book.

The first chapter of a book is usually an introduction of some type. Although you should read it first to get a feel for the book, you may wish to index it last. After you read chapters with more detailed discussion, you will be able to write more precise headings.

To choose entries, proceed as you did in your overview: read chapter titles, heads, and subheads. Look for topic sentences in each paragraph, as well as words that are boldfaced or italicized. Mark the words you consider important with a colored marker. It's better to mark too many entries rather than too few.

A book index doesn't necessarily include every occurrence of a word or phrase that you have marked. Entries should refer only to significant discussions of a topic. For instance, in a book on twentieth century presidents, you would include information on Eisenhower's approach to foreign policy. However, you would not include a reference to a statement like this: "President Truman, like Eisenhower after him, was beset by many problems."

Like all rules, this one is not hard and fast. Some books, like biographies and histories, require the inclusion of names and minute details that might be legitimately omitted from other types of books. Deciding what to include and what to exclude is the hardest part of indexing. Do Mi Stauber shares her techniques for identifying and phrasing concepts in her article, "Jewels in the Cavern," reproduced in chapter 4.

Forest and Tree Entries

When you begin to write index entries (phrasing headings is discussed in the next section), you should make two kinds of headings; I like to call them forest and tree entries. Forest entries are for the broad, general concepts discussed in a chapter. Tree entries are for the narrower topics and detail.

Write the general (forest) entries for the chapter first. This builds the index structure quickly and gives you a feeling of accomplishment. It's similar to getting past writer's block: you get something on that blank screen (or 3 x 5 card) that gives you the creative impetus to continue.

Next, make the specific (tree) entries. Read through the marked chapter and make an entry for each important point you noted.

In many cases, you can make both forest and tree entries simultaneously. That is, you write the general entries with their associated subheadings and create new entries by "flipping" the heading and subheading. This technique is discussed in more detail on page 28. If the book is very detailed, however, you may find that you will need to make several passes through the chapter to be sure you don't omit details.

Avoiding Bias

While you are choosing and phrasing headings, try not to let any personal prejudices show through. Professional indexers keep a neutral attitude while creating the index; that is, they index the content of the book—not their own ideas about what the book should have said. (See the bibliography for Bell's article on bias.)

Nouns and Noun Phrases

Index entries are always written in noun form. Descriptive phrases are used as subheadings modifying the noun phrase, as shown in the next example.

> assault in public schools
>   corporal punishment considered as, 249
>   defined, 169
>   student assaults on school personnel, 169

In selecting terminology for headings, choose the word that the reader is most likely to think of. For example, if the subject being indexed is expenditures for child protective services in the United States, the user of your index is not likely to go to the E's for expenditures or to the U's for United States. Rather, the reader would most likely look under the C's for child protective services.

Be as specific as possible in selecting headings. If your keywords are too generalized, the reader will have less chance of going directly to the subject under discussion. For example in a book discussing acquisition policies in public and academic libraries, use the headings "Public libraries" and "Academic libraries," rather than the more general term, "Libraries," and include a cross-reference from "Libraries" to the more specific terms. (Cross-references are discussed in chapter 5.)

Usually main headings begin with a noun, but sometimes an adjective-noun phrase is more specific and more likely to be how the reader looks for the information (for example, "Public libraries" rather than "Libraries").

Singular vs. Plural

Entries may be in singular or plural form, depending on the meaning conveyed. That is, if the topic is one that indicates something that is countable, use the plural form:

forks
knives
ladles
spatulas
spoons

Use the singular form if the heading is a collective term or answers the question "how much:"

cutlery
kitchenware
silverware

Some publishers prefer to indicate plural forms in parentheses:

eye(s)
gland(s)
kidney(s)

This practice results in some awkward constructions:

antibody(ies)
glomerulus(i)

It is better to use the singular or plural form as appropriate without parentheses.

Linked (Precoordinated) Headings

Sometimes entries involve two closely related terms linked with "and:"

colleges and universities

libraries and librarians

However, if the author distinguishes between "colleges" and "universities" in providing information about academic programs or if there is a large amount of information about librarians as distinct from libraries, these concepts should not be linked. Instead each concept should be a main heading linked with a See also reference.

Paraphrasing Entries

Not all entries can or should be used exactly as they appear in the book or article. For example, the book may have the heading "Sources of Roosevelt's Diplomatic Activism." Your card would look like this:

Roosevelt, Franklin Delano
    diplomatic activism, 22–25

Sometimes headings in the text contain more than one indexable concept: "From the Rogers Act to World War II" or "Acheson's Background and Appointment." This is how these headings would look:

Acheson, Dean
    appointment as secretary of state, 36–37
    qualifications for office, 35–36

Rogers Act, 19–20

World War II, 22–23

Consistency

If the book you are indexing is long, or if you are working on a magazine index over the period of a year, it is easy to forget how you phrased a heading previously. Be sure to check your earlier work as you progress through the index so that you keep all entries to one concept together under one heading. For example, you might make a heading "Drug abuse" one time and "Substance abuse" another time. Alphabetizing your cards periodically makes it easy for you to check your headings. If you are indexing on a computer, your indexing program will alphabetize entries for you.

Subheadings

Subheadings (also called subentries) are entries that are subordinate to a main heading. Subheadings indicate different aspects of a main heading. If you have more than five or six page references (or other forms of locators) attached to a main heading, you should use subheadings to break up the long list of references, as shown in the next two examples:

Middle East, 64, 72, 76–77, 146–65,181,
    196, 281, 282, 300, 302, 313

Middle East
    Eisenhower administration, 146–65, 181
    oil fields, 64, 72, 313
    Reagan administration, 76–77, 281, 282,
        300, 302

Relationship of Headings to Subheadings

Subheadings are logically related to the headings they modify, as shown in the many examples in this chapter. Many indexers (and publishers) also want subheadings to be grammatically related—a longstanding indexing tradition. The heading/subheading combination is supposed to form a phrase:

Angiography
    adverse effects of
    of aorta
    in atherosclerosis
    contrast media for

Showing the grammatical relationship results in subheadings bristling fore and aft with prepositions, articles, and conjunctions; words that are becoming better known as "function words."[*]

Alphabetizing Subheadings

This leads to one of the great controversies among indexers: how to alphabetize subheadings that begin with function words. Should the initial function word be ignored, or should it be alphabetized? Indexing textbooks and style guides have recommended for many years that initial function words should be ignored and that the subheading should be alphabetized on the first *significant* word of the entry. This practice, however, is confusing to index users who may be unaware of this filing convention commonly used by indexers and publishers. The following examples show both styles of alphabetization.

---

[*] Wellisch, Hans H. "Function Words in Subheadings," *Key Words* 1, no.4 (1993):8–10.

Function Words Alphabetized

Atherosclerosis
    as risk factor in ischemic stroke, 993
    in coronary artery disease, 994
    plaque from
        ischemic stroke caused by, 1024
        spinal cord ischemia with, 1082
        TIA caused by, 994

Function Words Ignored in Alphabetization

Atherosclerosis
    in coronary artery disease, 994
    plaque from
        ischemic stroke caused by, 1024
        spinal cord ischemia with, 1082
        TIA caused by, 997
    as risk factor in ischemic stroke, 993

Indexing standards recommend that indexes should contain as few function words as possible at the beginning and end of subheadings, and, if function words are used at all, they should be alphabetized just as any other word. Whether or not this advice will be accepted by the publishing community remains to be seen.

Starting the subheading with a key word also avoids the problem of how to alphabetize function words:

Atherosclerosis
    coronary artery disease and, 994
    plaque from
        ischemic stroke caused by, 1024
        spinal cord ischemia with, 1082
        TIA caused by, 997
    risk factor for ischemic stroke, 993

Phrasing and Editing Subheadings

The wording of subheadings is important because readers must be able to find specific facts quickly and easily. Select the first word of the subheading carefully so that it represents the main idea of the subheading. Compare the following examples. The second one conveys the same information directly and economically.

ordination
    examples of rituals from the 19th century,
       182

ordination
    rituals from 19th century, 182

As you add subheadings to the index, you may discover that you have added several similar entries. Try to combine related subheadings into a single entry with multiple page references (but no more than 5–7 page references per subheading), as shown in the next set of examples:

Preliminary Entries

arithmetic assessment
    addition and subtraction, 476–78
    addition calculation, 465, 468
    conservation, 425–26
    conservation task, 475–76
    flexible interviewing, 443–47
    interviewing, 495–96
    goal of, 415–17
    number facts, 469–70, 483–86
    standardized measurement, 441–43
    standardized tests, 463–65, 491–95
    student's ability to learn, 419–20
    student's learning potential, 496
    subtraction, 473
    thinking processes, 485, 487
    thinking strategies, 442–43, 447–56
    types of student thinking, 418–19

Edited Entries

arithmetic assessment
    addition and subtraction, 465, 468,
      473, 476–78
    conservation task, 425–26, 475–76
    interviewing, 443–47, 495–96
    goal of, 415–17
    number facts, 469–70, 483–86
    standardized tests, 441–43, 463–65,
      491–95
    student's learning ability, 419–20,
      496
    thinking processes, 418–19, 442–43,
      447–56, 485, 487

Running-in a Single Subheading

You may discover while editing that you have just one subheading for some headings. If you feel that the subheading is necessary to the meaning of the entry, you can "run it in" after the heading, or you can rephrase the heading to incorporate the subheading, as shown next.

configuration file
    changing, 4–7

becomes

configuration file, changing, 4–7

ordination
    women, 39–40, 183

becomes

ordination of women, 39–40, 183

Some indexing software can help with editorial chores, such as joining orphan subheadings to their headings, as well as spellchecking, and verification of cross-references. But no software can phrase the entries for you. There is no substitute for printing and reading the entire index.

Page Range vs. Subheadings

Including the page range after the main heading when the topic is also subdivided by subheadings is another controversial topic in indexing. Some indexers argue that main headings followed by sub-headings should not include the page range after the main entry. Others feel that it is helpful to give the page ranges anyway in order to indicate the extent of the coverage. I agree with the latter view because it shows readers how much information exists on a specific topic without forcing them to read through a possibly lengthy list of subheadings.

This issue is even more relevant in medical and scientific books. For example, supposed a book on pediatrics discusses measles on pages 89–90. Is it better to make a single main heading for measles or to include subheadings?

Measles, 89–90

Measles
    clinical findings, 89
    diagnosis, 89
    pathology, 89
    treatment, 89–90

I would argue for including the subheadings because they inform healthcare workers of the exact topics covered in the text. If readers are looking for some other aspect of measles, they need not bother to consult the text. Otherwise, they can turn to the indicated page and be assured of finding what they want.

Bringing Information Together

Subheadings are also used to group together similar entries that readers might otherwise overlook. For instance, in a computer manual, some readers might always think of "function keys" and never look under "keys." Other readers might think of "keys" first, not knowing what specific types of keys are available. The idea is to group together specific terms under a main heading, and also make main headings for the specific topics themselves.

cursor keys, 7, 32

function keys,9, 33

keys
   cursor keys, 7, 32
   function keys, 9, 33

For that reason, subheadings are often used as main headings as well as subheadings. This process is also known as flipping entries, inverting entries, or double-posting.

Inverting or Flipping Entries (Double-Posting)

As shown above, headings can be used as subheadings and vice versa. This practice allows readers to find the item of interest whether they think of the topic from either the general or the specific viewpoint. For example, if you have marked "ordination of women" in the text, you would make the following two entries:

ordination
   women ministers, 188–89, 202

women
   ordination as ministers, 188–89, 202

One thing to consider while writing index entries is whether to flip the entries at the time you make the original heading or wait to double-post the entries during a second pass through the chapter. Although it is easy to flip entries when you are using indexing software, you may forget to flip some entries when you are concentrating on writing main headings. Your indexing may be more accurate if you make two or more passes through the marked chapter. On the first pass, write the main headings (forest entries). On the second pass, go back and make main headings from the subheadings you included under the forest entries. It may be necessary to make a third pass through the material to write main headings for even more specific topics.

Levels of Subheadings

You are not limited to one level of subheading. Many scientific, legal, scholarly, or technical works are so detailed that they require more than one level. The following example shows two levels of subheadings:

```
Abdomen
    abscess of
        computed tomography of, 417, 417
        drainage of, 1229, 1319–1320
        ultrasonography of, 374–375, 375–377
    acute
        complications of, 976–977
        diagnostic tests for, 973–974
        intraoperative management of, 974–975
        postoperative care of, 975–976
        surgery for, 974
    anatomy of, 1439
```

It is easier for the reader to find the desired information if you limit subheadings to one or two levels (the main entry plus one or two levels of subheadings). Your choice in this matter also depends on the publisher's preference.

Classification in Indexes

One of the purposes of an index is to bring information together, as noted earlier. The indexer must take care, however, not to become too obsessed with gathering every bit of related information into larger chunks, a practice known as classification. For example, in a book on farm and ranch animals, you might make a classified entry like this:

```
cattle
    bulls
        reproductive system, 36, 44–46, 93
        sexual activity, 99–102
    cows
        artificial insemination, 98–101
        estrous cycle, 62–64
        reproductive system, 121–125, 198–203
```

Some indexers argue that classification has no place in an index. In *Indexing from A to Z*, Wellisch (1995) says that no matter how reasonable a classified index may seem to the indexer, the reader may not understand the thought process the indexer used to create the classified list of subheadings. Wellisch argues that instead of classifying subheadings, you should make main headings for each of the subheadings.

There are several options for unclassifying the "cattle" entry. You can convert the sub-subheadings and keep the "cattle" entry, or you can make a See reference from "cattle" to "bulls" and "cows."

> cattle
>   artificial insemination of cows, 98–101
>   bull reproductive system, 36, 44–46, 93
>   cow reproductive system, 121–125, 198–203
>   estrous cycle of cows, 62–64
>   sexual activity of bulls, 99–102

In this "flattened" example, the main problem is that the reader has to scan each subheading to see whether it pertains to bulls or cows. In a situation like this, it is probably better to make the following entries:

> bulls
>   reproductive system, 36, 44–46, 93
>   sexual activity, 99–102
>
> cattle. *see* bulls; cows
>
> cows
>   artificial insemination, 98–101
>   estrous cycle, 62–64
>   reproductive system, 121–125, 198–203

Whether or not you classify subheadings depends on the nature of the book. If the entire book is about raising cattle, you probably would not even make a main heading for "cattle." Instead, you would make main headings for the specific breeds of cattle and other topics, such as "artificial insemination," "reproduction," and "nutrition."

If the book is about farm and ranch animals in general with a few paragraphs or one chapter about cattle, then you would be justified in making an entry for "cattle" as well as specific breeds, if they are discussed.

I believe that classified entries work well for the reader as long as the subject being subdivided is not too general and as long as the entry does not continue for column after column. I think readers appreciate having all relevant information gathered together in one place. It is just as easy for a reader to scan a list of classified subheadings as it is for him or her to scan a long list of unclassified subheadings. I think it is preferable to make classified entries rather that leaving the reader guessing whether he or she has found all the relevant information that might otherwise be scattered throughout the index. For an excellent discussion of classification, see Moys' article listed in the bibliography on page 35.

Recording Entries

Recording entries for either the 3 x 5 card method or computer-assisted method is very similar. You must make a separate card or computer record for each heading and accompanying subheading (and sub-subheadings, if any). For example, you would have to make four cards (or computer records) for the following index segment:

```
keys
    cursor keys, 2–7
    function keys
        Fl (help key), 3–34
        F2 (save key), 3–36
    special purpose keys, 2–5
```

Note: The page references shown in this and the following examples represent the type frequently found in computer manuals, that is, the first number represents the chapter and the number following the hyphen is the page number

The first card is:

```
keys
    cursor keys, 2-7
```

The second card is:

```
keys
    function keys
        F1 (help key), 3–34
```

The third card is:

```
  keys
      function keys
          F2 (save key), 3–36
```

The fourth card is:

```
  keys
      special purpose keys, 2–5
```

Why shouldn't you put as many entries on a card as possible? For ease of alphabetization. If you have only one entry per card, you can sort your cards into exact alphabetical order without having to check multiple entries spread over one or more cards. This also helps prevent errors when you are typing the final version of the index. If you have more than one entry per card, you might accidentally omit a subheading or type it in the wrong order, which means retyping one or more pages. Computer-assisted indexing programs require separate records for each entry for the same reason.

If you are concerned about wasting paper, one indexer recommends marking out the old index entry and using the back of the card, flipping cards over to use tops or bottoms of the same side, using different color ink to record new entries, or as many ways as you can think of.

Indexing Names

When do you include names in an index? Generally, you include names if there are several sentences of discussion about a particular person or place. As usual, it depends on the type of book, the audience of the book, and the author's wishes.

Usually, you will omit names that are merely listed, for example, as attendees at a particular event. In biographical works, these minor "mentions" may be considered important, so you will need to consult with the editor or author on how to handle them.

In scientific and technical books, names are frequently cited in the text, but these are not usually indexed since complete bibliographic information is provided for each chapter. For social science and humanities works, however, names may comprise a large part of the index.

Names in Scholarly Works *

Scholarly books (in the social sciences and humanities) often include many name citations within the text, like this (Garcia, 1998). Should these be included in the index? These names are important because scholarly authors base their research on other scholars' research. Readers are likely to track this process by looking up names in the index; the name of the researcher who specializes in a subject may be just as familiar an access point as the subject itself. It is also a reality that scholars' tenure and reputations can depend on being cited in the works of others. Some indexers and publishers therefore feel that they should be indexed. On the other hand, they should not take precedence over subject entries when space is at a premium.

The final decision, of course, is made by the publisher, and scholarly publishers do vary a great deal in their policies. It is common to index all names cited in the text. Some publishers specify that names cited as part of a sentence should be indexed (As Mueller has discussed in her latest work (1999)...), while names cited in parentheses (Cohen, 1975) should not. Some publishers do not want them indexed at all.

When the citations occur in footnotes or endnotes, the rule about what to index in these locations applies. Substantive material only should be indexed. This means that an author cited in a note should be indexed only if quoted or discussed substantively; recommended further reading on the topic is not indexed.

Two last points about scholarly name citations: when last names appear in the text without first initials, the indexer must add the initials, found by scanning the bibliography or endnotes. When cited names (as opposed to names discussed as subjects) are indexed in a scholarly book, they usually do not receive subheadings.

---

* Thanks to Do Mi Stauber (with assistance from Barbara Cohen), who contributed this section.

Forms of Names

When you index biographies, historical books, or other works that contain many names, dealing with names can become a challenge. You may find that the author refers to the same person in different ways throughout the book. In some extremes, the author may cite names inaccurately. You will need to contact the editor to see how to handle such situations.

Another common problem is that the author may refer to a well-known person only by last name. You will need to check your reference shelf (or your local library) for the full name of the person.

You may encounter many other problems with personal names, such as non-English names, compound names, royalty or nobility, saints and church officials, persons without surnames (like Aristotle), pseudonyms (i.e., Mark Twain for Samuel Clemens), geographical names—the list is endless.

Fortunately, there are several reference works that can help you deal with names: *Anglo-American Cataloguing Rules, The Chicago Manual of Style, Indexing Books,* and *Indexing from A to Z,* and several articles listed in the "Further Studies" section below. Chapters 8–11 also discuss reference tools to help indexers in various subject specialties.

Separate Name Indexes

Periodical indexes (magazines, journals, newsletters, and newspapers) usually have separate name indexes. These types of indexes are explained in chapter 7, "Indexing Special Formats."

Further Study

American Society of Indexers. *Subheadings: A Matter of Opinion.* Port Aransas, TX: American Society of Indexers, 1995.

Anglo-American Cataloguing Rules. 2d edition. Chicago: American Library Association, 1984.

Bell, Hazel. "Bias in Indexing and Loaded Language." *Indexer* 17, no. 3 (1991): 173–177.

Bertelsen, Cynthia D. "Indexing Chinese Names: Some Basic Guidelines." *Key Words* 6, no. 1 (1998): 16–17.

The Chicago Manual of Style. 14th ed. Chicago: University of Chicago Press, 1993.

Diodato, Virgil. "User Preferences for Features in Back of Book Indexes." *Journal of the American Society for Information Science* 45, no.7 (1994):529–536.

Ingraham, Holly. *People's Names: A Cross-Cultural Reference Guide to the Proper Use of Over 40,000 Personal and Familial Names in Over 100 Cultures.* Jefferson, NC: McFarland & Company, Inc., 1997.

Moys, Elizabeth M. "Classified v. Specific Indexing: a Reexamination in Principle." *Indexer* 20, no.3 (1997):135–136, 153–155.

Muvany, Nancy. *Indexing Books.* Chicago: University of Chicago Press, 1994.

Thompson, Jean A. "What's in a Name: Beyond *Webster's Biographical Dictionary*, Part One: Personal Names." *Key Words* 6, no. 2 (1998): 1, 12.

Thompson, Jean A. "What's in a Name: Beyond *Webster's Biographical Dictionary*, Part Two: Corporate Names." *Key Words* 6, no. 4 (1998): 6–9.

Wellisch, Hans H. *Indexing from A to Z.* 2d ed. New York: Wilson Company, 1995.

Wellisch, Hans. "Subheadings: How Many Are Too Many?" *Key Words* 1, no. 6 (1993): 12–13.

Wittmann, Cecelia. "Subheadings in Award-winning Book Indexes: a Quantitative Evaluation." *Indexer* 17, no. 1 (1990): 3–6.

Chapter 4
Jewels in the Cavern:
The Special Challenges
of Scholarly Indexing

Do Mi Stauber

As an indexer of scholarly monographs and essay collections, I never know what I'm going to be learning about next: The transformation of an occupational drinking culture...Air power and coercion in war...Economies of race and gender in early modern England...Authenticating culture in interwar Japan...Immigrant Jews in the Hollywood melting pot.

Indexers do a lot of talking and writing about the mechanics of indexing: how we alphabetize, how we word subheadings. These details are extremely important, but only because they provide the structure that leads the reader to the content. I want here to write about that content.

So I've received the page proofs of my next scholarly book. They're sitting on the page rack in front of my computer screen, looking as dense and pristine as always. They contain a whole world of ideas. I have the breathless feeling that I always experience at the beginning of an index, wondering what the authors are going to say, how they're going to say it, where the text is going to take me. Sometimes that breathless feeling, I must admit, has a tinge of panic in it.

I find myself hoping that the authors will just spell it out for me, outline their main points (and then use them to name their chapters), tell me the final conclusion and exactly how they're going to prove it. Sometimes I wish that my balance of clients and jobs was more heavily weighted towards textbooks. Textbooks, though they come with their own particular problems and challenges, are definitely easier to index!

Textbook organization is right out on the surface. Chapters are usually parallel subsections of the main subject. For instance, in a human development text there are sections on Infancy, Childhood, Adolescence, Adulthood and

Old Age, with various areas of development discussed in each section. This structure carries over into the index. As I read the book, I'm likely to be able to stand back and record straightforward messages from the author: "I am now going to define five approaches to psychotherapy."

Scholarly books, of course, vary in their degree of structure. Some scholarly authors do spell out their arguments overtly, explain the exact relationships between the concepts they're discussing, and construct clear chapters or sections that correspond to these arguments and concepts. The structure, on the other hand, may not be outlined clearly, and the organization may be organic. Either type of book may be thrown together without much care—or it may be brilliantly written.

The authors in an organically organized book intend, not just to present information, but to give the reader an experience. The book follows the flow of their thoughts as they explore their topic in greater and greater depth. I read along from concept to concept, finding myself immersed by turns in rich historical context, intricate personalities, details of literature, and philosophical implications. All of this gradually weaves a more and more connected tapestry, until suddenly I realize that I'm inside a completely woven whole—it all falls together, and I have not just been told what the authors are trying to communicate, I have experienced it for myself. That is why, even though textbooks are much more remunerative and much easier to index, I keep indexing scholarly books. And as I stare at my pile of page proofs, I ready myself to take a deep breath and plunge into the world of the text, trusting that I will swim in it and understand it.

Plunging In

How do I go about swimming in a text? How do I choose entries and organize them, when the authors are not handing them over on a silver platter?

The first requirement is patience. I have to trust that the indexing process, like the text, will circle back and overlap itself. This may entail reading a section several times, or letting it stew in my mind before I make any entries.

I allow myself to use very wordy headings on my first time through. I can get stuck too long looking for the perfect concise wording for a concept that may not even have come clear in my own head yet; it's best to enter, for instance, "toxic waste plants are located in neighborhoods of poor people and people of color." This pulls together all of the entries about that topic, allowing me to see the connections and plan the final locations for those entries. In this case, there turned out to be a whole cluster of entries under just that concept. Eventually it became a main heading: "Polluting facilities siting in poor and minority communities."

In each paragraph or section, I figure out what the main idea is. This may seem obvious, but in some books it isn't clear without a very careful reading. This is because the many concepts in the book are woven together throughout the text, and extracting one of them tends to bring the whole tapestry of the book out with it.

This extraction process must be done, though. I need to understand for myself what the author is talking about. And a clear fix on the main idea makes it possible to "cover" each section of text with index headings. A main idea heading will include all of the pages in a section; important concepts that are discussed in relation to the main idea can often be indexed with the main topic as a subhead. For instance:

> This precarious balance between universal ideals and national spirit was also implicit in the philosophical cosmopolitanism circulating in the Taisho institutions of higher learning where Kuki received his education. As an intellectual movement, cosmopolitanism was closely associated with the literary and artistic Shirakabaha (White Birch Society), but also with the Japanese dissemination of German idealist thought, particularly neo-Kantianism.

This paragraph turned up in the middle of a discussion of Kuki's education, mixed with a description of the various philosophical/cultural/political movements in Japan during his lifetime. It took a close look to see that Cosmopolitanism is the main topic, and that this paragraph is the (unannounced) beginning of a three-page section about that topic. Thus I "covered" the next three pages with "Cosmopolitanism." Kuki's education, Taisho period, Neo-Kantianism, and Shirakabaha, some of which are important ongoing topics in the book, were all ancillary entries, using cosmopolitanism as a subhead when appropriate.

Sometimes the authors are just saying whatever seems interesting about the work, time period, or general subject that they're discussing, in willy-nilly order. It helps to remember this when trying to break a large section into subheadings!

The Knee Bone's Connected to the Leg Bone

Transitions between concepts can be clear and obvious, announced by section headings. More often, though, these section headings are decorative or metaphorical rather than explanatory—billboards on the side of my journey, not signposts telling me where I am. The concept transitions are likely to be subtle, leading the reader painlessly along the author's path. But as an indexer I have to find the divisions between topics, making enough structural sense of the text to break it down into index entries.

For example, a chapter in the Japanese culture book is called "Encounters Across Borders." After a careful preliminary reading, I discovered the following divisions in the first part of the chapter: an introduction about Kuki's intellectual influences; Kuki's studies in Europe; a description of neo-Kantianism and a discussion of why it was attractive to people in interwar Japan, leading to Kuki's relationship to this movement. None of these sections were clearly announced by the author; I had to figure them out. What first appeared as a long, undifferentiated discussion (with a decorative title) emerged as a logically organized narrative. The sections outline the progression in time of Kuki's ideas, with excursions when necessary into the wider historical and scholarly context. It makes perfect sense and leads the reader to an organic understanding of Kuki's philosophy—but the indexer has to do some work to translate the concepts into structured index elements.

What's It All About, Alfie?

In any book, the main topic or topics are extremely important. These concepts are the ones under which the whole book could be indexed, the ones to which every heading I make will relate in some way. This relationship is assumed, and therefore the topic will either not be indexed at all as a main heading or have very few subheadings. Even when it is only implicit in the index, it is the lodestone of the whole structure.

As I wrote this article, I kept trying to put the main topic section first. Surely, given the centrality of this concept to the indexer, I shouldn't leave it until last! But in organically organized books, the main topic may not emerge until later in the process.

A textbook's main topic is obvious. It is the field about which the text is giving information: English literature, Early childhood curriculum, U.S. foreign policy. An academic book, however, can be much more complicated. For one thing, the main focus is likely to be a much more specific problem or situation: racial terminology in Elizabethan culture, whole language versus phonics in reading instruction, U.S. drug war strategy. And the concept that becomes the structural center of the scholarly index is not the situation being studied, but the argument the authors are making about that situation. How was racial terminology used in Elizabethan culture, and why? What is the best way to teach reading? I may need to read the whole book before I understand this main concept.

In some ways, the entire process of indexing an academic book that is organized organically is one of discovering, uncovering, the author's main message. Whereas indexing a textbook is like driving along a highway, following the road signs and knowing my destination, the academic process is like searching through a dark network of caverns. I dig out kernels of meaning, threads of connection, with intuition as my guide. As I unearth them, I record them as best I can.

Eventually I find myself feeling completely lost. About to tear my hair out with frustration, I decide that I have no idea what the author is saying (and on a bad day, that I'm really a terrible indexer and after ten years will now be found out!)

At this very disheartening moment, I turn to my editing notes and start writing out my confusion. Here is what I wrote at one such point: "Okay, she's saying that during this period the dark/light dichotomy was racialized, and that this happened because England was starting its imperialist expansion and that made people (men) anxious about their national identity and about difference in general, and this anxiety was usually expressed through focus on gender differences as well as racial ones."

As I read over this summary, which usually persuades me that I understood more of the text than I thought I did, all of the bits of treasure I've found and recorded fall into their places in relationship to it. I have suddenly understood how the caverns are constructed: I perceive the author's main point. If I have been careful and complete in my recording—if my intuition has been true—I may be almost finished at this point. If not, I may need to go back and refashion the connections more clearly.

In this example, writing the paragraph made me realize which themes run through the whole book, gave me my main heading "Imperialist expansion," and made me stop trying to put everything under Gender and allow myself to make more specific gender entries.

In Conclusion

An author wrote to me recently, "I had no idea that the notion of 'dual consciousness' popped up in so many different places, and I consider the compiling of these references under a single heading to be your original contribution to the book. As is the whole index, really." Scholarly indexers, in our wanderings through these caverns of thought, can add richness to the text by finding connections not made by the author. This way of indexing needs a high tolerance for uncertainty. We are more than mechanical structure-makers and detail-recorders. We are all explorers, with all of the challenge and creativity that go with that occupation.

Chapter 5
References

Types of References

Two types of references are common in most indexes: page references (also called locators) and cross-references. Page references show the reader exactly where a topic can be found. Cross-references lead the reader to entries that might be otherwise overlooked, or point out additional information on a subject.

Page References

Page references are the page numbers where the entries can be found. In books and magazine articles, you indicate either separate page numbers or a range of pages if the discussion goes on for more than one page. Page references are usually separated from the index entry by a comma (this depends on the publisher's style preferences). Some technical manuals separate entries from page references by two or more blank spaces. When an entry has more than one page reference, the page numbers are also separated from each other by a comma:

    Education
        free marketplace model, 80–81, 83
        objective inquiry and, 99–101
        openness to criticism, 102–103

In the run-in style (formats or styles for indexes are described on page 54), the main entry is followed by a colon and subheads are separated with semicolons:

    Education: free marketplace model, 80–81;
        objective inquiry and, 99–101, 102–103;
        openness to criticism, 102–103

Pages in many technical manuals are numbered nonconsecutively; each chapter begins with the chapter number followed by a page number. That is, chapter one is numbered 1–1, 1–2; chapter two is numbered 2–1, 2–2; and so on.

Page Ranges

When a topic is discussed on more than one page, an en dash (represented by a hyphen on typewriter and computer keyboards) separates the beginning and ending pages, as in the example above. An en dash is half the width of an em dash. The em dash is the width of the letter M.

To designate page ranges in manuals using the chapter/page style of numbering mentioned above, use "to" between pages, e.g., 1–1 to 1–3. The page references in some manuals are separated with an em dash (1–1—1–3), but this style is potentially confusing to the reader.

Abbreviating Page References

How page numbers are abbreviated in ranges depends on the style manual you are following. Some publishers want no abbreviations at all:

    certification
        alternative routes, 56–57
        ethical considerations, 199–201
        requirements for principals, 135–136
        suspension of, 102–103

The Chicago Manual of Style would abbreviate these references as follows:

    certification
        alternative routes, 56–57
        ethical considerations, 199–201
        requirements for principals, 135–36
        suspension of, 102–3

The editor of the book you are indexing should provide you with the preferred style for abbreviating page ranges.

Other Types of Locators

You may also encounter materials in which item numbers (or paragraph numbers) are the primary means of identification, such as bibliographies. In this case, you will need a note at the beginning of the index to indicate that numbers refer to item numbers rather than page numbers. Page references for magazines and newspapers are discussed in chapter 7.

References to Notes

You should index footnotes or endnotes if the information they contain goes beyond bibliographic citations for the material being discussed. Sometimes notes contain information that is considered peripheral to the main topic in the text but may be valuable to readers who are exploring every facet of a particular topic. Indicate such references by adding "n" to the page reference if there is only one note on the page.

> Yarborough, Ralph
> candidacy for Texas governor (1952), 37, 412n

If there are many notes on the page, add the number of the note you are indexing, e.g.:

> Yarborough, Ralph
> candidacy for Texas governor (1952), 37, 412 n. 8

Show references to multiple notes as follows:

> Yarborough, Ralph
> candidacy for Texas governor (1952), 37,
> 412 nn. 8, 10

Cross-References

The most common cross-references in book indexing are the See reference, the See also reference, and the general See also cross-reference.

See References

The See reference leads readers from a term that is not used to the proper entry. Here are some uses for See references:

1. From an abbreviation or acronym to the spelled-out form of the name, or vice versa, depending on which is better known:

   > American National Standards Institute. *see* ANSI

2. From a synonym that is not used as the heading to the equivalent or related word that is used as the main heading:

   > rubella. *see* German measles

3. From a term embedded in a compound heading:

    > university libraries. *see* college and university libraries

4. For inverted headings or headings that have more than one word, consider terms other than the first word:

    > disabilities, learning. *see* learning disabilities

5. From variant forms of a person's name or a geographic location, such as pseudonyms, women's married and single names, place names that have changed, or from trade names to generic names in pharmaceutical and medical works:

    > Advil. *see* Ibuprofen
    > Ceylon. *see* Sri Lanka
    > Constantinople. *see* Istanbul
    > Davis, Nancy. *see* Reagan, Nancy
    > Twain, Mark. *see* Clemens, Samuel

6. From popular to technical terms or scientific names in a technical or scientific book (or vice versa, depending on the author's choice of terminology):

    > Lactrodectus mactans. *see* black widow spider

Be careful not to make a See reference from a term to a main heading that you later decide not to use (a blind reference). Nor do you want the following situation:

> colleges. *see* universities

> universities. *see* colleges

Multiple See references are listed in alphabetical order and separated by semicolons:

> libraries. s*ee* academic libraries; public libraries; special libraries

Sometimes, as in the case of synonyms, it is better to list the page reference(s) under both terms rather than using a See reference. This is appropriate only if there are not many page numbers involved and no subheadings. This practice is also called double-posting.

See Also References

See also references lead readers from an existing entry to a related entry. For example:

> civil rights. *See also* African-Americans; integration; racism
>
> libraries. *See also* academic libraries; public libraries
>
> science. *See also* astronomy; biology; physics

Multiple See also references are listed in alphabetical order and separated by semicolons, as shown above.

Location of See Also References

See also references may follow the main heading (after any page references), or they may be listed as the last subheading of a group. Both styles are shown in the next two examples.

> constitutional rights. *see also* First Amendment;
>   Fourteenth Amendment
>   Bill of Rights, 16,17
>   curtailment of rights, 17
>
> constitutional rights
>   Bill of Rights, 16,17
>   curtailment of rights, 17
>   *see also* First Amendment; Fourteenth Amendment

It is generally better to place See also references after the main heading rather than the last subheading because readers start their search at the beginning of a main heading and work their way down the list. If they find what they are looking for before they reach the end of the list, they may never find the See also reference. Therefore, they are less likely to miss the reference to related material if it is placed immediately following the main heading.

Format and Punctuation of Cross-References

The examples in this chapter show the cross-reference separated from the entry with a period (.). Cross-references may be also be preceded by a comma, or enclosed in parentheses.

colleges. *see* universities

colleges, *see* universities

colleges (*see* universities)

The keyword, See, may be in upper- or lowercase letters. See also references are formatted and punctuated the same as See references.

Multiple See or See also references are listed in alphabetical order and separated by semicolons:

Infections. *See* Bacterial infections; Fungal infections; Viral infections

Science. *See also* Astronomy; Biology; Physics

General See Also References

General See also references are used when you want to be sure that readers consult not just a general concept but also specific terms that are related to the general concept. If there are too many specific terms to list individually (making the index unnecessarily long), you can make a general statement about other topics to check:

Central America. *see also* names of specific countries

churches. *see also* names of specific churches and church leaders

organizations. *see also* names of specific organizations

Cross-References from Subheadings

In addition to the See and See also references from main headings, you may also make either kind of reference from subheadings as shown in the following examples:

cardiac arrest
    circulatory support in, 22–23
    myocardial ischemia during, 32
    outcome evaluation of, 18t
    resuscitation for. *see* cardiopulmonary resuscitation

kidney failure, chronic
    dietary limitations in, 269–270
    etiology of, 267–268
    transplantation for. *see* kidney transplantation

See Under and See Also Under References

See under and See also under refer readers to subheadings listed under main headings.

malignant peripheral nerve sheath tumors. *see under*
    nerve sheath tumors

outcome. *see also under* specific topics
    definition of, 178, 179–180
    pediatric. 202–203

These types of cross-references seem to be most common in medical or scientific books. Wellisch recommends against using them at all, and I agree.

Verifying Cross-References

Before you commit the index to its final form, check all your See references to be sure they refer to an actual entry with a page reference or subheadings (i.e., no blind references). Sometimes during the editing process you may delete main headings to which a See reference points, resulting in unintentional blind references.

A similar error to watch for is See also references that refer to each other, i.e., circular references. In this case, no page reference is attached to either entry. Also check that the wording of all cross-references match the main headings to which they refer. If you are using one of the better stand-alone indexing programs, the software will assist you with cross-reference verification.

Chapter 6
Finishing Touches

After you have completed making and recording entries, several tasks remain. These include alphabetizing the index, editing headings and subheadings, selecting a format or style, and committing the index to paper (or disk).

Alphabetizing the Entries

Main headings are alphabetized in either letter-by-letter or word-by-word order. Letter-by-letter alphabetization ignores spaces between words and treats the entire entry as if it were one long word. Word-by-word alphabetization considers each word letter by letter, starting over after each space. The table below shows the difference between the two styles:

Letter by Letter	Word by Word
New Amsterdam	New Amsterdam
Newark	New Brunswick
Newberry	New England
New Brunswick	Newark
New England	Newberry
Newfoundland	Newfoundland

Your publisher's style guide will determine which sort order you use. If the choice is left to you, however, you should try both systems to see how they affect the index. If headings that the reader might expect to find together are being separated because of the sort order, select the system that will work best for the reader.

One quirk of the letter-by-letter style is the rule that alphabetization starts over when you encounter a punctuation mark. This practice can result in the separation of similar terms as shown in the next example.

DNA, recombinant
DNA, ribosomal
DNA, single-stranded
DNA recombinant proteins. *See* **Recombinant proteins**
DNA repair

You may wish to change the order of the alphabetic arrangement if you feel that your readers will miss information that is separated because of the punctuation rule.

Alphabetization is far more complicated than it may seem at first glance. Some of the problems with alphabetization are mentioned briefly in this section. You can obtain further guidance from the filing rules set forth by various standards organizations and other bibliographic bodies. Some of these publications are listed at the end of this chapter. NISO is publishing a new standard, *Alphabetical Arrangement of Letters and the Sorting of Numerals and Other Symbols*, by Hans Wellisch. Also refer to discussions in Mulvany's *Indexing Books* and Wellisch's *Indexing from A to Z*.

Initial Articles and Prefixes

Initial articles in titles of literary or artistic works are usually transposed, as recommended by the ISO 999 standard:

Old Man and the Sea, The

Articles in foreign languages can be difficult to handle if you are not familiar with the language. Wellisch presents an excellent chart of articles in a variety of languages in his *Indexing from A to Z*.

Initial articles in place names are not transposed and the article is not disregarded. If you encounter these types of names, do your reader a favor by making a *See* reference from the inverted form of the name to the initial article:

Hague, The. *See* **The Hague**

Initial articles in personal names are not disregarded.

    El Greco
    Forbes, Lady Adelaide
    Hobhouse, John Cam
    La Fontaine, Jean de

Prefixes (particles) in personal names in foreign languages can also be difficult to work with. If you are indexing a book with these kinds of names, refer to Wellisch or the *Anglo-American Cataloguing Rules*.

Numbers and Symbols

Numbers and symbols have traditionally been alphabetized as if spelled out. In some works in the social sciences and humanities there may be very few numbers or symbols. You can probably sort them as if spelled out, but you may also place them at the beginning or end of the index in addition to the spelled-out forms. You should mention in the introductory note where the numbers and symbols can be found.

In technical books and computer manuals, numbers and symbols may have considerable significance and should not be sorted as if spelled out. Sorting numbers numerically is no problem, but symbols are another matter since there is no real standard for their placement. You can leave symbols in the default ASCII order (used by personal computers), accept the order used by your indexing software, or devise a sort order that is satisfactory to both you and the publisher.

Subheadings

Subheadings are alphabetized the same as for main headings. See page 24 in Chapter 3, "Writing the Index," for a discussion of sorting function words in subheadings.

When to Alphabetize the Index

If you are working on 3 x 5 cards, you can either keep the cards in page number order until you have completed all the entries, or sort them into alphabetical order as you complete each chapter (or each entry for that matter). If you are indexing a book for which some (or all) of the pages are not yet numbered, you will most likely want to keep the cards in entry order (page number order). If you choose to sort them alphabetically, you must be willing to re-sort the entire index in order to change the page references when they are known.

Another reason you may wish to keep the cards in page number order is to recheck your entries for each page to make sure you have not overlooked an entry you intended to make. Although it is a good idea to go back through the manuscript and check each entry against the marked pages, you may not have the time available to do so.

If you are using good indexing software, you can keep the entries in alphabetical order as you work and sort the entries into page number order when you need to check them or change the page references. Indexing before the final page numbers are known is discussed in more detail in chapter 7.

Editing the Index

Editing the index is not something that occurs only after you have completed writing entries. Editing is an integral part of the entire indexing process. As you progress through the marked manuscript, you will find new topics that need to be integrated with existing entries. Entries that you made earlier may have been minor discussions of a topic that will need to be rephrased after you read a major discussion of the same topic.

The same is true for subheadings. When you discover new material that belongs with an existing subheading, you will need to add page references to the existing entry and possibly reword the entire subheading in light of the new information.

Nonetheless, you still need to read and edit the index before sending it off to the editor. The following checklist details the tasks involved in editing the index.

An Editing Checklist

♦ Proofread
   ◊   You can proofread entries at the same time as you are performing other editing tasks. This is second nature for some indexers, while others insist that proofreading should be a separate step. Most likely you won't have time to read through the index more than once, especially if it is a long one.

♦ Spell-checking
   ◊ It is difficult to catch every spelling error in proofreading. Use the spell-checker in Cindex or your word processor to help with this task.
♦ Check main headings for consistency
   ◊ Are some of the main headings in singular form and others in plural form?
   ◊ Is some other inconsistency keeping headings in separate groups? Can these headings be combined or should they truly remain separate?
   ◊ If the index is large, you may wish to take advantage of the summary view in Cindex or the Headings utility in Macrex to look at just the main headings.
♦ Read for sense
   ◊ Have you expressed the concept in the most understandable form?
   ◊ Is the phrasing concise but still understandable?
♦ Subheadings
   ◊ All the items above apply to subheadings as well. See page 25 for examples of editing subheadings.
♦ Double-posting
   ◊ Check *See* cross-references to determine if you should double-post the entry instead of using a cross-reference.
♦ Page references
   ◊ If you discover that some of your page references are incorrect, check related entries for incorrect references as well. You can do this by sorting the index into page number order (or by using the group feature of indexing software to find a certain range of pages for checking).
   ◊ Ensure that you have formatted page numbers in the style required by the publisher. Again, your indexing software can help you enter page numbers accurately and format them correctly.
♦ Cross-references
   ◊ Verify that *See* references refer to an entry that actually appears in the index (i.e., no blind references).
   ◊ Check that the wording of See and See also references match the text to which they refer.
   ◊ Ensure that See also references are not circular, that is, they do not refer to each other without having page references or subheadings at either location.
   ◊ Good indexing programs will check these things automatically and print a list of inconsistencies for you to check.

When you have completed editing the index, you are ready to print it in the desired format for shipping to your editor.

Formats or Styles for Indexes

There are two common formats for the back-of-the-book indexes: indented style (or entry-per-line) and run-in (or paragraph) style. Always check with the editor before you begin an index to determine the required style. If a publisher prefers some format other than the standard ones, the editor should give you a style sheet describing the requirements.

Indented Style

The indented style is most commonly used for scientific or technical books. Although it requires more space, it is easier for readers to find specific subheadings. The indented style has been used in most of the samples in this guide.

        colleges and universities
            academic freedom, 97–98, 101–102
            classroom evangelicalism, 77–78
            president's role, 101–102
            student's reactions to faculty, 10
            trustees' role, 6–7

Run-In Style

The run-in style is used in most general (trade) books, biographies, the humanities, and scholarly publications. The main heading is usually followed by a colon and subheadings are separated by semicolons. Although there are some hybrid versions of the run-in style that allow you to use sub-subheadings, there are rarely used. (See page 61 for an example of a modified run-in style index.) Therefore, if you are forced to use the run-in style, you are limited to one level of subheading for the index.

        colleges and universities: academic freedom, 97–98;
            classroom evangelicalism, 77–78; president's role,
            101–102; student's reactions to faculty, 10; trustees'
            role, 6–7

Typographical Considerations

You will find almost as many different typographical conventions in indexes as there are publishers. The goal is to make the index easy to read.

Whether or not the first word of the main entry is capitalized depends on the style guide you are following (and whether the word is a proper noun). The existing and proposed indexing standards recommend lowercase entries. All subheadings begin with lowercase letters except for proper nouns.

Mulvany's *Indexing Books* contains a table that compares style requirements of several publishers and standards.

Electronic Index Files and Typesetting Codes

Many publishers require indexers to submit indexes in electronic form, usually on disk, but also by e-mail or modem. They may also require the indexer to insert typesetting codes. As for style or format requirements, the editor will supply you with the required codes. The best indexing programs can insert these codes for you automatically.

Introduction to the Index

If your index uses special conventions, symbols, or anything else that may not be clear to readers, include an introduction in a paragraph at the beginning of the index.

Introduction

Page references for charts and tables are followed by a "t", that is, 151t. Photographs and illustrations are indicated by an "i", 134i. Maps are indicated by an "m," as in 28m. There are separate indexes for subject terms and authors' names.

An introduction for a magazine index is presented in chapter 7.

Index Preparation Methods

There are several methods for getting the index entries from scribbled notes on the manuscript to the final typed or printed version that you send to the publisher: the 3 x 5 card method, typing the index in a word processor, or making entries in stand-alone indexing programs.

3 x 5 Card Method

The traditional 3 x 5 card method may be the most comfortable method for someone indexing a book for the first time. Since this procedure was used in samples throughout chapters 3–5, it is only summarized here.

Type or print only one entry on each card. Alphabetize the cards as you proceed (unless you plan to check the cards against each page of the manuscript before you alphabetize them). When you have completed indexing the entire work, edit the entries. That is, combine page numbers, decide which subheadings are pertinent, whether or not the phrasing is correct, and finally, verify cross-references.

Although you have alphabetized the cards as you worked, it's a good idea to check the order of the cards before you begin typing. Then familiarize yourself with the required format (or style) and type the index. After typing the index, you must once again carefully proof the typed entries against the original cards.

If you are indexing a magazine or a collection of records or reports that will continue into the future, you will want to put the data on a computer as soon as possible, since this makes it easier to cumulate the index annually (or more often).

Word Processor Method

If you prepare the index with a word processor, you basically follow the same procedure as for 3 x 5 cards, except that you don't type the entries on cards. Each time you add a new page reference or subheading to an existing entry, use the find (or search) feature of the word processor to locate the proper entry and insert the new page number or subheading where it belongs.

Word processing is not very satisfactory for long books or cumulated magazine indexes, but it works well for documents that are short and straightforward and avoids the necessity for retyping pages and checking against the cards.

Stand-Alone Indexing Software

Since 1982, many specialized indexing programs have been developed by and for indexers, mostly for the IBM PC and compatibles. Generally they follow the traditional 3 x 5 card pattern, but they take care of the alphabetization, formatting, and printing. You can find a complete review of each of these programs in Fetters' *Guide to Indexing Software*.

The choice of indexing programs has recently improved. Cindex offers versions for DOS, Windows, and Macintosh computers. Another Macintosh program is HyperIndex. Macrex is available only in a DOS version, but a Windows version is under development. SKY Software has two Windows versions of indexing programs, the SKY Index for Windows (standard edition) and SKY Index Professional. For additional information or demonstration versions of these programs, contact the vendors at the following addresses:

Cindex:
Indexing Research
100 Allens Creek Road
Rochester, NY 14618
Phone: 716-461-5530
Fax: 716-442-3924
e-mail: info@indexres. com
http://www.indexres.com

HyperIndex
André de Tienne
4444 Sharon Lane
Indianapolis, IN 46226
Phone 317-274-2033
e-mail adetienn@iupui.edu

Macrex:
Wise Bytes
P.O. Box 3051
Daly City, CA 94015-0051
Phone: 650-756-0821
Fax: (650) 757-1567
e-mail: macrex@aol. com

SKY Index
SKY Software
6016 Oxpen Ct. Apt. 303
Alexandria, VA 22315
Phone: 703-921-9472/800-776-0137
Fax: 703-921-9472
e-mail: email@sky-software.com
http://www.sky-software.com

Further Study

American Library Association. ALA *Filing Rules*. Chicago: American Library Association, 1980.

Anglo-American Cataloging Rules. 2d. ed. 1988 revision. Chicago: American Library Association, 1988.

Fetters, Linda K. *A Guide to Indexing Software.* 5th ed. Port Aransas, TX: American Society of Indexers, 1995.

Mulvany, Nancy. *Indexing Books.* Chicago: University of Chicago Press, 1993.

Wellisch, Hans H. *A Guide to Alphanumeric Arrangement and Sorting.* Oxon Hill, MD: NISO, 1999.

Wellisch, Hans H. *Indexing from A to Z.* 2nd ed. New York: Wilson Company, 1995.

Chapter 7
Indexing Special Formats

The first six chapters cover most of the techniques you need for indexing a book. This chapter covers special cases in book indexing, such as biographies, and indexing before page numbers are known. Also discussed are nonbook materials: periodicals (journals and magazines, newsletters, and newspapers), electronic documents, and Web indexing. The bibliography at the end of this chapter lists many good articles about indexing special types of documents and materials.

Biographies

Biographies can be a special challenge to the indexer. After all, most of the book is about the minute details of one person's life. You certainly don't want to use that person's name as the only main heading and list all the rest of the book as subheadings under that name. But there are some subheadings, such as "birth of," "death of," or "personal characteristics," that do not easily fit elsewhere in the index.

This problem is partially solved by making entries under other people's names, such as the subject's mother, father, siblings, or whoever else played an important role. You can also make entries under headings for the biographee's career, hobbies, and other interests, and place names where he or she lived or visited. For example, if the person is a writer, you can make entries under the names of his or her works. If the subject is a politician, you can make entries under political campaigns, names of the agencies or government bodies, and other relevant topics.

If you cannot logically make a subheading fit under one of these categories, it is better to place too many subheadings under the subject's name than to hide them under some obscure heading that the reader may miss. As an illustration, the following excerpt is from an index I wrote for *The Journal of Thomas Moore*, a six volume set*. The entry for "Moore, Thomas," includes subheadings only for personal information that were not appropriate for main

---

* Moore, Thomas. *The Journal of Thomas Moore*, ed. Wilfred S. Dowden, 6 vols. (Newark: University of Delaware Press), 1983–1991.

headings. See also references from subheadings lead the reader to personal information that was too voluminous to include under Moore's name. Page references are indicated by ###. (Looking back at this index nine years after completing it, I can see that the phrasing could be more consistent and the subheadings could use more editing.)

> Moore, Thomas: admirers and petitioners of. *See* Admirers and petitioners; asylum in France. *See* France, TM's asylum in; attitude toward dying, ###; attitude toward his children, ###; Bessy's pet name for ("Bird"), ###; birthdays of, ###; busts of. *See* Portraits and busts of TM; caricatures of, ###; conversations. *See* Conversational topics, notable; criticized by Americans, ###; dahlia named for, ###; decision not to sing in presence of professional musicians, ###; early acceptance in society, ###; exaggerated newspaper accounts of his failing health, ###; fall suffered by, ###; farce about (*The Irish Lion*), ###; financial matters of. *See* Financial matters of TM; fit of weeping after singing "The Song of the Olden Times, ###"; his failing memory, ###; his mental decline, ###; his religious beliefs, ###; his singing debut in London, ###; his youthful appearance, ###; infected or inflamed leg of, ###; invitations to stand for parliament, ###; lodgings of. *See* Lodgings of TM; minor illnesses of, ###; muscular pains of; performances as "Peeping Tom" and "Robin Roughhead, ###"; poems to and about. *See* Admirers and petitioners; popularity of. *See* Admirers and petitioners; portraits of. *See* Portraits and busts of TM; recollection of eary serious illness, ###; reputation as a dandy, ###; Russell bequeaths his seal ring to, ###; shoulder injury of; Thomas Little as pseudonym for, ###; travels of. *See* Travels of TM; Trismagistus Rustifustius as early pseudonym for, ###; tumor in groin, ###; wedding anniversaries of, ###; wrist injury of, ###

It is customary to use the subject's initials when you are referring to him or her in subheadings, as shown above.

The "Moore, Thomas" heading is followed by 12 pages of "Moore, Thomas, works." The editor decided it would be more useful to gather all the works together in one place, especially since many of them were "squibs" published in newspapers, often anonymously or under a pseudonym. These entries serve as an example of the modified run-in style:

> Moore, Thomas, works—"Ah why that tear?," ###
> —"Alarming Intelligence," ###
> —*Alciphron*: completion of, ###; conception of, ###; included in new
>   edition of *Epicurean*, ###; research for, ###
> —"Believe me if all those endearing young charms," ###
> —*Fudge Family in Paris, The*: admirer talks to TM about, ###; lines about
>   Canning in, ###; lines about Lord Castlereagh in, ###; parody on,
>   ###; praise of, ###

Traditionally, subheadings in indexes for biographies or historical works have
been arranged in chronological order. Let your publisher and your conscience
be your guide in this case. If your audience is scholarly, they may expect to find
the subheadings in chronological order (usually page number order). If the
book is intended for a popular audience, they probably expect the subheadings
to be in alphabetical order.

As for any other index, go to the library and find a biography with a good index and use it as a template for your own index. Hazel Bell discusses the
challenges of indexing biographies in her booklet, *Indexing Biographies and
Other Stories of Human Lives*.

Indexing Books Before Pagination Is Known

Sometimes a publisher may ask you if you want to start working on an index
when the book is still in the galley proof stage (before page endings have been
determined). Although it may seem like a good idea to get an early start on
the index, it is actually more trouble than it is worth. Frequently, however,
publishers may be able to give you page proofs with the correct page endings
but without final page numbers. Although it is inconvenient to work without
final page numbers, it is not impossible. You will need to assign a temporary
page number that will identify the chapter and the page number. As with
technical manuals, you could use 1–1, 1–2, 1–3, etc. or some combination of
letters and numbers. When you receive the final page proofs, you will go back
and change the temporary page numbers to the final page numbers.

If you are indexing on 3 x 5 cards, you will need to keep the cards in page
number order until you are able to compare the temporary pages with the final page proofs. If you need to alphabetize the cards to be able to compare
similar entries, then you must be willing to re-sort them into page number
order.

If you are using an indexing program, the process becomes somewhat easier. The better programs allow you to work on the entries in alphabetical order, and then re-sort the index into page number order to make the final page changes. These programs have find and replace capabilities for automatically changing the temporary page numbers to final page numbers. The manuals for both of these programs contain suggestions for dealing with temporary page numbers.

Magazines and Journals (Periodicals)

There are two approaches to magazine and journal indexing. The more traditional method, the kind seen in indexes to large collections of magazines, such as the *Reader's Guide to Periodical Literature* or *Index Medicus*, is similar to cataloging books in a library. Rather than making a detailed analysis of each article as you would for each chapter of a book, you generally assign five to seven subject headings to each article. The title of the article (or a shortened form of the title) is used as the subheading, and the locator consists of the month and year (or volume and issue) plus page reference.

The second approach is to index periodicals the same as for books. In this style, the title of the article may be adapted to use as the subheading, or the indexer may write a more specific subheading without making any reference to the article title. The book-style indexing approach allows the index to reference topics that appear on a specific page instead of using the "shotgun" approach that simply gives the page range for the whole article, leaving the reader to search through the entire article to find the desired nugget of information." Nancy Mulvany discusses book-style magazine indexes in "Periodical Indexing" in *Managing Large Indexing Projects*, as listed in the bibliography.

Periodical indexes usually include separate author and subject indexes. An author index may consist of a simple list of names and locators, or it may contain the name of the article as a subheading to the author's name. The larger the collection of magazines indexed, the more need for article titles.

Indexing Decisions

Periodical indexes require many decisions about what should be included. Magazines may have sections on restaurant reviews (or listings of favorite restaurants in a city), brief news items or gossip columns, letters to the editor, book reviews, movie and theater reviews, music or record album reviews, and other type of information in addition to major articles. Before you start to index, you need to decide which of these types of information you are going to include in the index.

As usual, you will need to consult with the publisher or editor about what types of materials should be included. You will also need to include these decisions in an introduction to the index. The introduction to the five-year cumulated index for *Third Coast* magazine (created as a class project by indexing students at the University of Texas at Austin) is reproduced here as an example. You may not need such a detailed introduction for your index.

Introduction

This is a five year cumulative index to *Third Coast,* from its beginning in August, 1981 through July, 1986. The index consists of two parts: an author index and a subject index.

Subject Index: The terminology of the subject index is as specific as possible and is based on the authors' wording as much as possible. See references lead readers from terms that are not used in the index to the appropriate term. See also references lead readers to groups of terms that are related to each other.

Because *Third Coast* provides a large number of articles on art, music, and various types of reviews, there are some special considerations to be aware of.

Art terms: General articles about art are listed under the heading, Art. Articles about specific types of art are listed under the specific type, such as Painting, Sculpture, etc. There is also a separate heading for Artists, as well as listings for each type of artist, such as Painters, Sculptors, Women—Artists.

Music terms: Much like the terms for art, general articles about music appear under the term, Music. There are also headings for Musicians, Music Groups, as well as listings under the names of individual music groups, musicians, and types of music.

Reviews: Book reviews, movie reviews, and record reviews can be found only under those headings. There are no listings for individual books, records, or movies, unless some article that was not a review discussed a specific movie, book, or record.

Alphabetization: Entries are listed alphabetically word-by-word rather than letter-by-letter. For example, Air traffic is listed before Aircraft. Abbreviations and acronyms are listed as if they were words. MUDs file between Mud wrestling and Muehlen. Numbers are listed as if they were spelled out.

Abbreviations and Acronyms: Abbreviations and acronyms usually appear in the index with a See reference to the spelled-out form of the name, that is, NSA. *See* National Security Agency. The exception to this rule is if the acronym is better known than the spelled out form, such as AIDS rather than Acquired Immune Deficiency Syndrome.

Excluded Materials: Sections of the magazine not included in the index are gossip columns, advertisements and the following specific columns:

Architest
Letters to the Editor
Listings
On the Aisle
Short Takes
Wrestling in Review

Photographs and illustrations are not specifically indexed. That is, no special typography was used to designate photographs or illustrations. They can be located, however, by looking under the subject term or name you are interested in.

Locators

In the case of periodical indexes, you need to include the date of the issue, as well as the page number, since each monthly or quarterly issue of a magazine may begin with page one. The reader needs to know which issue to consult, as well as the page range.

Day care facilities
  Computers can't play by themselves, Feb. 1984, 44
  The dark side of the moon, Nov. 1984, 74–97
  Kinder gardens, Oct. 1983, 100–103

If you are creating an index for a collection of magazines, the entry should include the name of the magazine, as well as the title of the article and possibly the author's name. Sometimes magazine indexes include the volume and issue number as well:

Money
  International aspects
    Cooper, Richard N. A monetary system for the
      future. *Foreign Affairs* 63:166–184 Fall '84

Subject Authority Lists and Thesauri

Choosing subject entries for periodicals is different from choosing subject headings for books. Book indexes are usually prepared by one indexer who generally follows the author's terminology. If a new edition of the book is released, the new index, although it may be based on the old index, is unique for that book.

When you are preparing an annual or cumulated index for a magazine (or a collection of magazines), or for a collection of in-house reports that will continue to grow, choosing subject headings with consistency becomes more difficult for several reasons:

♦ There may be more than one indexer working on the project.
♦ The periodical articles or reports are multi-authored, so there is less consistency of terminology.
♦ The terminology changes over time.

A subject authority list (or subject heading list) can help you and fellow indexers maintain consistency throughout the index. An authority list contains subject terms for a particular area or discipline, such as education, medicine, or library and information science. Or a subject authority list may be general and all encompassing, such as the *Sears List of Subject Headings* or the *Library of Congress Subject Headings* used by many libraries.

Subject heading lists also indicate synonyms which are not to be used as headings. In addition, *See* and *See also* references indicate relations between terms. Sometimes they also include approved subheadings.

A thesaurus is a similar tool which is usually compiled by experts in a subject field and is more highly structured than a subject heading list.

Some thesauri and subject authority lists commonly found in libraries are listed below. In addition to thesauri, you can refer to periodical indexes published by some of the indexing and abstracting services, such as the Wilson Company *(Education Index, Social Sciences Index, General Science Index),* as guides for assigning subject headings.

Engineering Index Thesaurus (Engineering Index)
Library of Congress Subject Headings
Medical Subject Headings (MeSH) (National Library of Medicine)
PAIS Subject Headings (Public Affairs Information Service)
Sears List of Subject Headings (Wilson Company)

> *Thesaurus of ERIC Descriptors* (Educational Resources Information Center)
> *Thesaurus of Psychological Index Terms* (American Psychological Association)

If you are involved in setting up procedures for indexing magazines, a collection of reports, or other similar files, you need to decide whether you want to develop your own subject authority list or whether a thesaurus or list already exists that you can use for your own indexing. It is much easier to use or modify an existing thesaurus if possible. Developing and maintaining your own thesaurus is a time-consuming and expensive process—one that is rarely needed for most book or magazine indexes. If you feel you must develop your own thesaurus, refer to the works listed in the "Thesaurus" section of the bibliography.

Newsletters

Indexes for newsletters are a cross between book and magazine indexing. Most likely you will not use the title of articles as subheadings, or if you do, you may need to shorten them. As for magazine indexing, you will need to make decisions about what to include. Most likely, you will index everything published in newsletters except the advertisements.

Locators will be the same as for magazines, indicating either the month, year, and page(s), or the volume, issue, and page(s).

Newsletters generally require a separate author index, unless the newsletter is written entirely by the staff of an organization and no credit is given for individual articles.

Newspapers

The procedure for indexing newspapers is similar to that for magazines. You have to decide whether to use a thesaurus or to establish your own vocabulary authority list. In addition, you may also need to establish a name authority file since you will be dealing with a large number of names, depending on how many newspapers you are including in the index, and how many years you are covering.

As with magazines, you need to decide at the start what classes of information you will include. Sandlin, Schlessinger and Schlessinger* considered the categories shown below when making decisions for indexing the *Texarkana Gazette.*

Accidents	Government bodies
Advertisements	Holidays & festivals
Awards	Legal proceedings
Births	Letters to the editor
Book reviews	Library activities
Buildings	Marriages
Business & industry	Minority groups
Churches	Obituaries
Clubs, organizations	Photographs & clippings
Columns	Politics
Crime	Schools
Editorials	Sports
Fillers	Town agencies

In magazine indexes, you generally use the title of the article (or some form of the title) as the best means of specifically identifying an article. Newspaper headlines do not always convey the true sense of the article, so you will most likely need to phrase the subheading yourself.

The other major difference between magazine and newspaper indexes is the locator. You will need to devise a method that shows the month, day and year, section, column (optional), and page. You may also want to include some designation for photographs, charts, and other graphics. For example, you could include a "type" indicator after the date, section, and page references to show what type of graphic is displayed In the example below, "P" represents photo. For the reader's ease of use, you should explain in the introduction to the index what the abbreviations above the column represent.

---

* Lesley McGee Sandlin; June H. Schlessinger, and Bernard S. Schlessinger. "Indexing Smaller-Circulation Daily Newspapers." *Indexer* 14, no. 3 (1985): 184–189.

	Date	S	P	Typ
Drug Abuse				
emergency rooms overloaded with cases	6/12/93	B	2	
mayor presents Service Award to teens	8/15/93	A	1	P
treatment program established	9/10/93	B	6	

As for any other index, you may find it helpful to look at other newspaper indexes before starting your own. Also, the articles listed at the end of this chapter contain many helpful suggestions and examples.

A wonderful resource for newspaper indexers is available online at http://metalab.unc.edu/journalism/indexing.html, where Barbara Semonche has published her chapter on newspaper indexing, "Newspaper Indexing Policies and Procedures" from the book, *News Media Libraries: A Management Handbook.* This site also contains a link to a large bibliography on newspaper indexing http://www.sun-site.unc.edu/journalism/indexbib.html.

Electronic Documents

CD-ROMs are a good example of the type of electronic documents indexers may encounter. In some cases, the indexer may prepare the index in the usual fashion using a stand-alone indexing program. Instead of page references, however, you may use special codes that indicate individual paragraphs. When the publisher receives the index file, their software will insert the links between the special codes in the index and the matching text on the CD-ROM. In other cases, the indexer may need to embed index entries directly into the electronic text using codes specified by the publisher. Garry Cousins explains this process in his article, "Conceptual Indexing for CD-ROMs: Beyond Free Text Searching."[*] (This article is supposed to be accesible on AusSI's Web page, but the link was not active at the time of publication.)

Computer software and hardware publishers frequently ask indexers to embed index entries directly into the documentation files. This is usually an extremely time-sensitive operation. The writer(s) and editors tend to make changes up to the last minute, but the indexer has to have the final files in order to embed the entries. An alternative is to index the document from a paper copy using stand-alone indexing software and then to embed the entries after the final editing of the index is complete. Either the indexer can embed the entries, or

---

[*] Cousins, Garry. "Conceptual Indexing for CD-ROMS: Beyond Free Text Searching." *Australian Society of Indexers Newsletter* 20, no. 7 (1996): 4–6.

she can provide the index printed in order of the locators along with a marked up manuscript showing where the index entries should be embedded. Mulvany discusses the ramifications of embedded indexing in her *Indexing Books*. Jan Wright also discusses embedded indexing, plus the indexing of other types of electronic files in her article, "How to Index Online," available as a PDF file on her Web site (http://www.mindspring.com/~jancw).

Online help indexing is a related type of electronic indexing, except that "keywords" (main entry plus subheading) are embedded in online help files and then compiled into an index (online help file, familiar to any user of Microsoft Windows-based computers). See Jan Wright's article, "Working with Windows Help Keywords," available at her Web site noted above, for more information. Other articles on indexing help files can be found in the "Electronic Document" section of the bibliography on page 73.

Web Indexing

Another form of electronic document indexing is Web indexing. Types of Web indexes range from the traditional back-of-the-book format to Web rings, subject trees, and many others. No doubt you could consider the underlying structure of each Web site and its links to other pages in the site as an index.

In 1997 I had the opportunity to write my first Web index. The following excerpt is from an article that originally appeared in *The Indexer*.*

The U.T. Policies and Procedures Web Index

For many years, I have maintained an online database (TxPoly) for the policies and procedures of the University of Texas at Austin, including the text of the policies, the tables of contents, and the indexes. The Web index is simply a conversion of most of the TxPoly database. Instead of being an index of other Web sites, it is a book-style index with links to a book that has been converted to electronic format. Although I converted the policies and procedures text files to HTML files, that part of the procedure is not described here.

Even though TxPoly is a very simple Web site, there were still many design decisions to be made: what size the files should be, what the "home page" should look like, how to move from one file to another, and how to format the

---

* Fetters, Linda. "A Book Style Index for the Web: The University of Texas Policies and Procedures Website." *Indexer* 21, no. 2 (1998): 73–76.

text and index. Before beginning to code the files, I spent a lot of time looking at the underpinnings of the ASI Web page (www.asindexing.org), especially its index, as well as the Regents Rules Web site. (The Regents Rules are part of the TxPoly online database, but the Web site is maintained separately.)

File Size

Two policies and procedures manuals are covered in the Web site. Separate indexes are provided for each manual, as well as a combined master index. The original indexes were contained in three large files. After mounting the index however, friends told me that the indexes took too long to load into browsers. Accordingly, I split each index into several smaller files, with several linking methods enabling easy transitions between index files.

File Names and Directories

All coding and designing can take place on your own computer. After coding, you can view the files in your browser and test the links. The only links you can't test while offline are links to other Web sites.

Fortunately you can keep all the files in one folder (directory) without worrying about the name of the directory on the Web server where they will eventually reside.

Creating the Index

The index can be produced with your usual indexing program. I converted the existing index files from the old TxPoly database to Cindex files. I decided to use the original locators as visual cues to the section numbers. (See the example on page 71.) I used the same section numbers for the links and anchors, as described in the next section.

Any of the popular indexing programs (Cindex, Macrex, or Sky Index Professional) can insert the HTML codes for the index main headings and sub-headings using their code table capabilities. You still have to insert the coding for individual links and anchors for the locators. You can avoid retyping these codes, except for the actual anchor/link name, by storing the codes in the user-defined function keys, macros, keywords, abbreviations, or acronyms available in these programs.

Building Links

By far the most difficult part of the project was inserting the links between the index entries and the paragraphs to which they pointed. Fortunately, this project had a built-in structure that was established many years ago. I was able to use the section names for anchors. No matter what names you use, the links have to be inserted in the index entries and the anchors have to be inserted into the matching text file.

The following example shows the codes used for indenting the index entries and the links for locators and cross-references. I've indented the subheadings to make the text easier to read. The <A NAME= code indicates an anchor, and the <A HREF= code indicates a link. When a user clicks on a link, the Hypertext Transfer Protocol (http) jumps to the matching anchor. (Main heads are shown in boldface for ease of identification.)

```
<DT><A NAME="daily"><I>Daily Texan</I>
  <DD>authority of Board of Operating Trustees over students and employees,
    <A HREF="h0409.html#h040919">HOP IV (4.09) (19)</A>
  <DD>editorial manager, <A HREF="h0409.html#h040910b">HOP IV (4.09) (10) (b)</A>
  <DD>election of editor, <A HREF="h0409.html#h04097">HOP IV (4.09) (7)</A>
  <DD>relationship with Journalism Department, <A HREF="h0409.html#h040910b">HOP
    IV (4.09) (10) (b)</A>
  <DD>relationship with Journalism Department, <A HREF="h0409.html#h040912">HOP
    IV (4.09) (12)</A>

<DT><b>Dangerous materials</b>. <I>See</I> <A HREF="combh.html#hazchem">Hazardous
  chemicals, fire code for</A>; <A HREF="combh.html#hazmatdis">Hazardous materials
  disposal</A>

<DT><b>Dean's Fellows</b>, <a href="h0310.html#h0310b2">HOP III (3.10) (II) (B)</a>

<DT><b>Deans</b>. <I>See also</I> <A HREF="combt.html#vpdean">Vice president and dean of
  graduate studies</A>
  <DD>established schools and colleges, consultative committee for selecting,
    <A HREF="h024.html#h0243">HOP II (4) (3)</A>
  <DD>evaluation of, <A HREF="h025.html#h025">HOP II (5)</A>
  <DD>new schools and colleges, consultative committee for selecting,
    <A HREF="h024.html#h0244">HOP II (4) (4)</A>
```

You can look at these files in detail at www.utexas.edu/policies/hoppm/.

Checking Links

This is a time-consuming process in this type of Web page where you have hundreds (maybe thousands!) of links. I believe there are programs that will check links for you, but I checked mine all by hand.

Transferring Files

My ISP had a file transfer program (FTP) available for downloading, which was easy to use. Once the addresses and passwords required to connect with the Web server are in place in the FTP program, it's just a matter of pointing at the file(s) you want to transfer and clicking on the arrow that transfers the files from your hard disk to the server.

Helpful Software

HTML Assistant Pro 97

Although there are many Web design programs available, all I wanted and needed was a program that made it easy to put codes into the file. Since I wanted to name each anchor and link individually, I didn't want to use a program that hides the code from the user.

HTML Assistant Pro makes most the codes available on button bars or drop-down menus. You point and click where you want a code to go, or you can select a chunk of text and have the proper starting and ending codes inserted. Any time you want to see the fully formatted file, you can bring up an internal viewer, or call up your own browser. Pro 97 also allows you to open a large number of files at the same time. You can also make global replacements through multiple files, one after another.

Contact Brooklyn North Software Works (www.brooknorth.com) for more information.

Cindex/Macrex/Sky Index Professional

As noted above, any of these programs can insert the coding for the index main headings and subheadings using their code table capabilities. You can use function keys or macros, keywords, abbreviations, or acronyms to insert anchor/link coding.

Third-Party Software

There are programs that can insert HTML codes in your uncoded index files. One of these is HTML Prep from Leverage Technologies (www.LevTechInc. com). Another program is Webix available from Dwight Walker, who also has a training course for Web indexing (www.wwwalker.com.au).

Sources of Information

ASI's Web site contains a basic introduction to Web indexing along with a list of Web index examples. The Australian Society of Indexers (AusSI) Web site has an excellent list of relevant Web sites and other links of interest. You could also join ASI's Web Indexing Special Interest Group (SIG) (contact Kevin Broccoli at brocindx@in4web.com), or you could join the WINDMAIL list (Web Indexers' Mailing List). Sign-up instructions and the scope of the list can be found at AusSI's Web site (http://www. zeta.org.au/~aussi/). Several articles are listed in the "Web Indexing" section of the.

Further Study

Biographies

Bell, Hazel. *Indexing Biographies and Other Stories of Human Lives*. Occasional Papers on Indexing, no.1. London: Society of Indexers, 1992.

Bell, Hazel. "Indexing Biographies: the Main Character." *Indexer* 17, no. 1 (1990): 43–44.

Cookbooks

Bertelsen, Cynthia D. "A Piece of Cke? Cookbook Indexing—Basic Guidelines and Resources." *Key Words* 7, no. 1 (1999): 1, 6–12.

Grant, Rose. "Cookbook Indexing: Not as Easy as ABC." *American Society of Indexers Newsletter* no. 8 (1990): 1, 4.

Electronic Documents

Cousins, Garry. "Conceptual Indexing for CD-ROMS: Beyond Free Text Searching." *Australian Society of Indexers Newsletter* 20, no. 7 (1996): 4–6.

Fillmore, Laura. "Beyond the Back of the Book: Indexing in a Shrinking World." *Key Words* 3, no. 3 (1995): 16–20.

Lathrop, Lori. "Considerations in Indexing Online Documents," *STC Intercom*, January 1996.

Lathrop, Lori. "Indexing with Doc-To-Help: an Overview." *Key Words* 3, no. 1 (1995): 1, 27, 30.

Mauer, Peg. "Embedded Indexing in FrameMaker." *Key Words* 6, no. 5 (1998): 1, 6–8.

Mauer, Peg. "Embedded Indexing: What Is It and How Do I Do It?," *Key Words* 6, no. 1 (1998): 14-15.

Ventress, Alan and Louise Anemaat. "The Banks Papers on CD-ROM Project at the State Library of New South Wales." *LASIE* 26, nos. 1–3 (1995): 18–27.

Wright, Jan C. "How to Index Online." *Indexer* 20, no. 3 (1997): 115–120. (An expanded version of the article is downloadable from http://www.mindspring.com/~jancw.)

Legal Publications
Callow, M. "Producing an Index to Legal Periodicals in the Foreign and Commonwealth Office Library using Cardbox." *Program* 19 (1985): 251–261.
Moys, Elizabeth, et al. *Indexing Legal Materials.* Occasional Papers on Indexing, no. 2. London: Society of Indexers, 1993.
Smith, Nigel. "Journal Indexing: Compiling the *Legal Journals Index.*" *Learned Publishing* 3, no. 3(1990): 162–167, 170–176.
Thomas, Dorothy. "Law book indexing". In *Indexing Specialized Formats and Subjects,* edited by Hilda Feinberg. Metuchen, NJ: Scarecrow Press, 1983.

Magazines and Journals
Callow, M. "Producing an Index to Legal Periodicals in the Foreign and Commonwealth Office Library using Cardbox." *Program* 19 (1985): 251–261.
Cornog, M. "Out of the Shoebox and into the Computer: Serials Indexing 1975–1985." *Serials Librarian* 10 (Fall 1985–Winter 1986): 161-168.
Gibson, John. "Indexing of Medical Books and Journals." *Indexer* 13, no. 3 (1983): 173–175.
Mulvany, Nancy and Dorothy Thomas. "Periodical Indexing: Design, Management, and Pricing." In *Managing Large Indexing Projects.* Port Aransas, TX: American Society of Indexers, 1994.
Raper, Richard. "Indexes for Journals." *European Science Editing* no. 49 (1993): 5.
Smith, Nigel. "Journal Indexing: Compiling the *Legal Journals Index.*" *Learned Publishing* 3, no. 3(1990): 162–167, 170–176.

Medical Publications
Blake, Doreen, et al. *Indexing the Medical and Biological Sciences.* Occasional Papers on Indexing, no. 3. London: Society of Indexers, 1995.
Lennie, Frances and Alexandra Nickerson. "Indexing Medical Works." *Key Words* 2, no. 2 (1994): 1, 12–16.
Wyman, Pilar. *Indexing Specialties: Medical.* American Society of Indexers (in publication).

Newspapers
Ahmad, Nazir. "Newspaper Indexing: An International Overview." *Indexer* 17, no. 4 (1991): 33–34.

Bakken, Lori and Michael M. Miller. *Guide to Indexing "The Forum."* Fargo, ND: North Dakota State University Library, 1992.

Kilcullen, Maureen and Spohn, Melissa. "Indexing a Local Newspaper Using dBASE IV." Indexer 20, no. 1 (1996):16–17, 22

Knee, Michael. "Producing a Local Newspaper Index." *Indexer* 13, no. 2 (1982): 101–103.

Koch, J. E. "Newspaper indexing: planning and options." *Special Libraries* 76 (1985): 271–281.

Milstead, Jessica L. "Newspaper Indexing: the Official Washington Post Index". In *Indexing Specialized Formats and Subjects,* edited by Hilda Feinberg. Metuchen, NJ: Scarecrow Press, 1983.

Morris, Carla D. and Steven R. Morris. *How to Index Your Local Newspaper Using WordPerfect or Microsoft Word for Windows.* Englewood, CO: Libraries Unlimited, 1995.

Peterson, Candace. "Newspaper Indexing." In *Managing Large Indexing Projects.* Port Aransas, TX: American Society of Indexers, 1994.

Sandlin, Lesley McGee; June H. Schlessinger, and Bernard S. Schlessinger. "Indexing of Smaller-Circulation Daily Newspapers." *Indexer* 14, no. 3 (1985): 184–189.

Semonche, Barbara P. "Newspaper Indexing Policies and Procedures." In *News Media Libraries: A Management Handbook,* edited by Barbara P. Semonche. Westport, CT: Greenwood Publishing Group, 1993.

Semonche, Barbara. P. "Newspaper Indexing: in Search of a Solution." *Collection Building* 7, no. 4 (1986): 24–28.

Walker, A. "Creating a Newspaper Index: Microcomputers to the Rescue." *Wilson Library Bulletin* 61, (October 1986): 26–29.

Other Special Formats

American Society of Indexers. *Managing Large Indexing Projects.* Port Aransas, TX: American Society of Indexers, 1994.

Bruner, Katherine Frost. "On Editing and Indexing a Series of Letters." *Indexer* 14, no.1 (1984): 42–46.

Crystal, David. "Indexing a Reference Grammar." *Indexer* 15, no. 2 (1986): 67–72.

Falconer, John. "The Cataloguing and Indexing of the Photographic Collection of the Royal Commonwealth Society." *Indexer* 14, no.1 (1984): 15–22.

Preschel, Barbara M. "Indexing Encyclopedias." In *Indexing Specialized Formats and Subjects,* edited by Hilda Feinberg. Metuchen, NJ: Scarecrow Press, 1983.

Simpkins, Jean. "Indexing Loose-leaf Publications." *Indexer* 14, no. 4 (1985): 259–260.

Thesauri

Aitchison, Jean and Alan Gilchrist. *Thesaurus Construction: a Practical Manual.* 2d ed. London: Aslib, 1987.

Batty, David. "Thesaurus Construction and Maintenance: a Survival Kit." *Database* 12, no.1 (1989): 13–20.

Batty, David. "Words, Words, Words—Descriptors, Subject Headings, Index Terms." *Database* 11, no. 6 (1988): 109–112.

Booth, Pat F. "Thesauri—Their Uses for Indexers." *Indexer* 15, no. 3 (1987): 141–144.

Feinberg, Hilda. "Thesaurus in indexing and searching: a review." In *Indexing Specialized Formats and Subjects,* edited by Hilda Feinberg. Metuchen, NJ: Scarecrow Press, 1983.

Lancaster, F. W. *Vocabulary Control for Information Retrieval.* Arlington, VA: Information Resources Press, 1986.

Milstead, Jessica. "Thesaurus Software Packages for Personal Computers." *Database* 13, no. 6 (1990): 61–65.

National Information Standards Organization. *Guidelines for the Construction, Format, and Management of Monolingual Thesauri.* Oxon Hill, MD: NISO, 1993.

Townley, Helen M. and Ralph D. Gee. *Thesaurus-Making: Grow Your Own Word-Stock.* Andre Deutsch, 1980.

Web Indexing

Fetters, Linda. "A Book-Style Index for the Web: the University of Texas Policies and Procedure Website." *Indexer* 21, no. 2 (1998): 73–76.

Kilcullen, Maureen. "Publishing a Newspaper Index on the World Wide Web Using Microsoft Access 97." *Indexer* 20, no. 4 (1997): 195–196.

Shumaker, Lois E. "Indexing the California Home Page." *Indexer* 20, no. 3 (1997): 127–129.

Walker, Dwight. "AusSI Web Indexing Prize." *Indexer* 20, no. 1 (1996): 6–7.

Walker, Dwight. "AusSI Web Indexing Prizewinners." *Indexer* 20, no. 3 (1997): 121–124.

Walker, Dwight. "Web Indexing Prize 1997." *Indexer* 21, no. 1 (1998): 15–18.

Chapter 8
Humanities Reference Works

Cynthia D. Bertelsen[*]

The first indexes were of a humanities subject—religion. Today, indexers working with humanities subjects must be familiar with a large number of facets within disciplines unless they specialize in one area only. For the purposes of this article, the humanities are defined as art, literary criticism, music, philosophy, and religion; there are many other subjects (e.g., theater), hut space constraints limit the discussion. Each of these disciplines has its own manner of presenting research and theory, each has its own special terminology, and each actually merits an article of its own. Thus, the humanities indexer, who may not always be a subject expert, often finds it necessary to refer to a number of reference materials in order to clarify problems that arise during the indexing process.

Humanities terminology is often called imprecise.[1] This perceived imprecision stems from the nature of the humanities where value (rather than facts) is often the point of discussion. In addition, terms are redolent with many meanings; for example, think about "realism." While knowledge accumulation in the sciences tends to be cumulative (as Newton wrote, "If I have seen further ... it is by standing upon the shoulders of Giants."), in the humanities, knowledge accumulation tends to be different. Insight into the human condition, through perception and discussion, rather than through experimentation, is the norm. Studies on the information-seeking behavior of humanities scholars[2] and on classification and indexing issues in the humanities provide the humanities indexer with crucial information about user information needs.[3]

Problems in indexing the humanities can be similar, of course, to the problems found in other subject areas. However, humanities indexers tend to have more inconsistencies with names of persons, places, and corporate bodies, particularly when the volume to be indexed is multi-authored. In par-

---

[*] Reprinted with permission, from *Key Words*, the newsletter of the American Society of Indexers 5, no. 5 (Sep/Oct 1997): 11–15.

ticular, there are pseudonyms, variant titles of works, and group entities which need cross-referencing.

In the case of these group entities like "Minor prophets" or "Baby Ballerinas," to use Wiberley's examples, there are often cross references from the group names to the names of individuals in the group and vice versa. Schools of art, literature, and music and their practitioners need to be verified. Acronyms and abbreviations are not generally the problem that they are in social science and scientific indexing, but sometimes there are acronyms that nevertheless need clarification. For example, there are the numerous acronyms like GRSM and RAM in music.

The humanities indexer cannot be expected to have a full-fledged research reference collection at his or her fingertips, but an investment in some basic reference tools can save time in the long run and ensure crucial accuracy. The following discussion of reference tools for the humanities indexer presents a number of inexpensive materials (denoted by paperback versions) as well as items that will only be found in academic research libraries.

Choosing Reference Sources

To begin with, how should an indexer choose reference materials? The following criteria are guidelines[4] that are generally used by librarians in book selection:

1. Purpose and scope of the work: What does this work have to offer? What aspects of a subject does it cover? What is unique about it in comparison to others like it?
2. Authority of the author or publisher: Is this work produced by an authority in the field? Are the author's or publisher's other works well reviewed and/or listed in bibliographies for core library collections in the subject area?
3. Currency of the material: Is the material up-to-date? If the work has been published for some time, is it updated regularly?
4. Format of the material: Does the format make it an easy source to use?

The following reference tools, both basic core references and those grouped by problem area, were chosen because of their currency, placement in bibliographies for core collections for academic libraries, and their usefulness to the indexer who may not always be a subject expert. Some were suggested by indexers in response to a query on INDEX-L: I asked indexers on INDEX-L to share with me their favorite or most necessary reference materials for indexing specific subject matter. (Internet sources, unless the resource is an online version of print material, are not included here, due to questions about the authority of the compiler in some cases and accuracy of the information included in various World Wide Web sites.)

Core Resources

Many indexing problems faced by the humanities indexer can be remedied with what might best be called a core reference collection. Materials in this collection include tools to deal with general acronyms, names of well-known people both living and dead, and basic terminology for the humanities as a whole. One of the most basic, and inexpensive, tools is *The World Almanac and Book of Facts*,[5] published annually and therefore valuable for its currency. Names of politicians and celebrities and information on American history, geography, and descriptions of foreign nations, are included. Dictionaries of ideas are another source for the indexer who is not a subject expert. Two of the most recently published of these works are *The Hutchinson Dictionary of Ideas*[6] and *Dictionary of Theories,*[7] with a broad range of entries on a number of major concepts in human knowledge. An older work, the *Dictionary of the History of Ideas*[8] is also still a valuable resource. *The Columbia Dictionary of Modern Literary and Cultural Criticism*[9] provides 450 entries with explanations of common theoretical terms in the humanities. Of course, the legendary *Encyclopedia Britannica* should be part of the indexer's reference library, because of its major subject outline discussion articles as well as shorter entries on most of humankind's knowledge. The online version is particularly useful because of its search capabilities, which saves time for the busy indexer.[10] The *Library of Congress Subject Headings (LCSH)*,[11] while definitely limited in some of its more politically incorrect usages, does provide cross-referencing guidelines for terms.

Names, Organizations, and Places

Verification of names, and especially name order, is a constant problem for the humanities indexer, especially when the text covers non-Western societies or languages that are not written originally in Roman script. Consulting various country-specific dictionaries is necessary in these cases, but if the name in question is of a person, place, or organization that is in the current news, *Facts on File; World News Digest*[12] is a possible source, as is *The International Year Book and Statesmen's Who's Who: International and National*

Organizations, Countries of the Word, and 8,000 Biographies of Leading Personalities in Public Life.[13] General biographical dictionaries listing names of persons no longer living include *Merriam-Webster's Biographical Dictionary,*[14] *Webster's Biographical Dictionary,*[15] *Dictionary of American Biography,*[16] and *Dictionary of National Biography.*[17] For names of living persons, use *Chamber's Biographical Dictionary,*[18] *The Cambridge Biographical Encyclopedia,*[19] and the *Who's Who* series by Marquis.[20] Particularly useful is the *Proper Names Master Index,*[21] which contains information on over 200,000 proper names. Finally, if a person has been written about or is the author or editor of a book, the Library of Congress Authority File has information about the correct form of the name, which is found indirectly by examining library catalogs or OCLC's FirstSearch Service catalog, WorldCat.[22]

Apart from names of persons, names of organizations and geographical names also present trying problems at times for the indexer. A helpful reference for verification of names of organizations is the *Encyclopedia of Associations: An Associations Unlimited Resource: A Guide to More than 23,000 National and International Organizations.*[23] Geographical names sometimes must be verified for inclusion in indexes and Oxford University Press' new edition of the *Mayhew* dictionary contains up-to-date information on the changes that occurred after the break up of the Soviet Union.[24] Other favorites are the recently reissued *Merriam-Webster's Geographical Dictionary*[25] and the dated *Columbia-Lippincott Gazetteer of the World,*[26] good for historical reference.

Indexing of humanities-related works is also enhanced by the use of historical dictionaries related to the time period and geographical area discussed in works about art, literature, and music. For general historical information, the *Larousse Dictionary of World History* is a useful resource.[27] Most periods of history have their own dictionaries, such as *The Oxford Classical Dictionary.*[28] Countries also have specific historical dictionaries; see, for example, the *Dictionary of British History*[29] and the 2-volume set of the *Dictionary of American History.*[30]

Acronyms

Another indexing problem in humanities indexing is that of acronyms, although the problem is not as prevalent as it is in the social sciences and sciences. In many cases, authors assume that the reader knows the meaning of an acronym, which may not be the case at all. Hence, it is often up to the indexer to provide this information by using dictionaries of acronyms. One of the best sources for this problem, as it is for all of the subject areas discussed in this series of articles, is Gale Research's *Acronyms, Initialisms, and Abbreviations Dictionary*[31] and its companion volume *Reverse Acronyms, Initialisms, and Abbreviations Dictionary: A Companion Volume to Acronyms, Initialisms, and Abbreviations Dictionary with Terms Arranged Alphabetically by Meaning of Acronym, Initialism, or Abbreviation.*[32] For international acronyms, the Foreign Broadcast Information Service[33] has published a series of works on acronyms used in the press and media of certain geographical areas, including the Third World. Gale also publishes the *International Acronyms, Initialisms, and Abbreviations Dictionary.*[34] For humanities-related U.S. government agencies, notorious for their acronyms, there is the slightly outdated *Guide to Federal Government Acronyms.*[35]

Synonyms and Concepts

Very possibly the biggest issue for the humanities indexer is term selection, the inclusion of synonyms, and choice of suitable cross-referencing terms to fully capture the concepts discussed in a text. This terminology may not always be referred to by the author, but readers may be looking for it. The following subject-specific materials are possible sources for complicated indexing problems involving term selection concerning concepts, names, and so on:

Art

Perhaps the most comprehensive reference source on art is *The Dictionary of Art,* [36] published by Grove Dictionaries. With 41,000 articles, this incredible 34-volume dictionary is available in some libraries—and the 1075-page index received the H. W Wilson/ASI Award for Excellence in Indexing in May 1997. Other general references for the extremely broad field of the visual arts include the *Encyclopedia of World Art,*[37] *The Oxford Companion to Art,*[38] *The Oxford Dictionary of Art,*[39] and the *International Dictionary of Art and Artists*[40] (the first volume of this set concerns art in general while the second is a biographical dictionary of artists). Other art-related references of use to the indexer include the *Glossary of Art, Architecture, and Design Since 1945*[41] and *The HarperCollins Dictionary of Art Terms and Techniques.*[42] While biographical information on artists can be found in the books listed above, there are also many biographical dictionaries that are specific to historical time periods, geographical regions, or type of art, such as the *Dictionary of Contemporary American Artists,*[43] the *Biographical Dictionary of Japanese Art,*[44] or the *Dictionary of American Sculptors.*[45] Greenwood publishes a series of topical dictionaries on art; *Medieval Art* is one example.[46]

Literary Criticism

Literary criticism is also broad in scope, especially now that world literatures are becoming more mainstream than they have previously been. Authors' names, pseudonyms, characters, literary forms and genres, and critical movements are among those things that indexers must verify and create cross-references to and from. One of the more general sources is *Benet's Reader's Encyclopedia,* now in its fourth edition, with an emphasis on world literature including Asia, Russia, Latin American, and the Middle East.[47] The *Dictionary of Concepts in Literary Criticism and Theory*[48] and the *Dictionary of Literary Terms and Theory*[49] both provide detailed information on literary concepts, genres, and critical movements in the form of short essays. Also of importance for the indexer of literary criticism is the *Encyclopedia of Literature and Criticism,* which gives detailed overviews of many of the critical elements in the field.[50] The *Encyclopedia of World Literature in the 20th Century* is another source with a good international focus.[51] Many of these sources provide information about authors, but one of the more comprehensive sources for international author information is Gale Research's *Dictionary of Literary Biography,* [52] which now numbers over 181 volumes. Pseudonyms of authors can sometimes be an issue in indexing and the *Dictionary of Literary Pseudonyms in the English Language* is a useful source.[53]

Music

Music, in common with other disciplines in the humanities, covers a tremendous range of subject possibilities. Titles of works, composers' names, performers' names, theory, form, and notation all need to be verified. An excellent source for nearly all musical questions is the 20 volume *The New Grove Dictionary of Music and Musicians,* recently issued in paperback.[54] *The New Grove* includes biographical information, as well as information on musical concepts. There is also *The New Grove Dictionary of American Music,*[55] as well as numerous other titles in the Grove repertoire. An inexpensive alternative is *The Concise Oxford Dictionary of Music,* containing 10,000 entries.[56] Other sources for music include *Music Subject Headings,*[57] *Selected Musical Terms of Non-Western Cultures,*[58] the *Thesaurus of Scales and Melodic Patterns,*[59] and the *Dictionary of Terms in Music: English-German, German-English.*[60] Another interesting resource is *An Early Music Dictionary,* [61] with terms from early English manuscripts and useful for the indexing of Western music history.

Philosophy

Philosophy is considered to consist of five major areas of concern[62] and, like the other disciplines in the humanities, there are many reference resources concerned with the divisions within each area. A major general resource, including a supplement published in 1996, is the *Encyclopedia of Philosophy*[63] considered to be a definitive work, although somewhat biased toward the Western philosophical tradition. Less expensive alternatives are *The Oxford Dictionary of Philosophy*,[64] *A Dictionary of Philosophy*,[65] and *The Cambridge Dictionary of Philosophy*.[66] An interesting resource is *Talking Philosophy*, which is similar to *Rogets' Thesaurus* in format and provides the user with numerous cross-references to related terms.[67] Eastern philosophy is treated by the recently published *Companion Encyclopedia of Asian Philosophy*.[68]

Religion

Religion is so multifaceted that it is impossible to include here more than a sense of the types of general references available. The *Encyclopedia of Religion and Ethics,* albeit an old source, is still respected for verification of religious questions.[69] Another general resource includes the recently published *Man, Myth, and Magic.*[70] For each individual religion, there are large numbers of specific dictionaries and encyclopedias; examples of some of these more basic resources include *the Encyclopedia of Jewish Concepts,*[71] *The Blackwell Dictionary of Judaica,*[72] *Encyclopedia Judaica,*[73] the *New Catholic Encyclopedia,*[74] *The Oxford Dictionary of Saints,*[75] *The Oxford Dictionary of Popes,*[76] the *Dictionary of Quranic Terms and Concepts,*[77] the *Dictionary of Islam,*[78] and the *Encyclopedia of Islam.*[79] Also of help with names is the *International Biographical Dictionary of Religion,*[80] as are the many sect-specific biographical dictionaries available.

How to Find What You Need

If the materials listed here do not answer a specific question that arises, finding what you need when it comes to a specific indexing problem in a specific subject area is not always easy. K. G. B. Bakewell wrote a helpful article on basic references for indexers, since revised, which points out reference tools that aid indexers in the indexing process. The materials are arranged by type of material, i.e., directories, encyclopedias, and the like. However, perhaps the easiest way to find a particular reference book is to ask your local librarian or to take a look at standard bibliographies of reference books, such as the American Library Association's latest issue of *Guide to Reference Books*[82] and *ARBA (American Reference Books Annual) Guide to Subject En-*

cyclopedias and Dictionaries.[83] Several library collection selection tools provide useful information,[84] and the *Dictionary of Dictionaries*[85] and *Kister's Best Encyclopedias*[86] can also narrow down your search for the appropriate reference source.

Doing an online search of FirstSearch can be fruitfull or fruitless, depending on what terms you use in the search. (see note 22). *Books in Print*[87] provides information on books currently in print.

Summing Up

Indexers have a number of problems to deal with while indexing humanities texts. Name verification for persons, organizations, and places are among those problems, as are problems with acronyms. Term selection and cross-referencing of concepts are the most important issues facing the humanities indexer, who has a wide variety of general and subject-specific reference tools to which to turn. Although the terminology of the author is always the first choice of the indexer, it is often necessary to create cross-references to and from the author's terms to others that might occur to the index user This is where is behooves the indexer to have a good idea of where those terms are defined, if the author doesn't provide that information.

Notes

[1]Stephen E. Wiberly, Jr. "Subject Access in the Humanities and the Precision of the Humanist's Vocabulary," *Library Quarterly* 53, no.4 (1983): 420–435.

[2]Elaine Broadbent. "A Study of Humanities Faculty Library Information-seeking Behavior," *Cataloging and Classification Quarterly* 6 (1986): 23–37; Sue Stone. "Humanities Scholars: Information Needs and Uses," *Journal of Documentation* 38 (1982): 292–313; Stephen Wiberley and W. G. Jones. "Patterns of Information Seeking in the Humanities." *College and Research Libraries* 50 (1989): 638–45.

[3]Derke Wilton Langridge, *Classification and Indexing in the Humanities* (London: Buttersworths, 1976) ISBN 0408707771.

[4]William A. Katz, *Introduction to Reference Work,* vol.1, 6th ed. (New York: McGraw-Hill, 1992), 24–29. ISBN 0070336385.

[5]*The World Almanac and Book of Facts* (Mahwah, NJ: World Almanac Books, annual). ISBN 0886878004 (paperback).

[6]Anne-Lucie Norton, *The Hutchinson Dictionary of Ideas* (Oxford: Helicon, 1995). ISBN 1859860508 (paperback).

[7]Jennifer Bothamley, *Dictionary of Theories* (Detroit, MI: Gale Research, 1993). ISBN 18734477058.

[8]Philip P. Wiener, *Dictionary of the History of Ideas: Studies of Selected Pivotal Ideas.* 4 vols. (New York: Scribners, 1973–1974). ISBN 0684164183 (paperback).

[9]Gary Hentzi, *The Columbia Dictionary of Modern Literary and Cultural Criticism* (New York: Columbia University Press, 1995). ISBN 0231072430 (paperback).

[10]Access *Encyclopedia Britannica* through http://www.eb.com. There is a free trial period, and then an inexpensive monthly fee after that.

[11]*Library of Congress Subject Headings,* 19th ed., 4 vols. (Washington, DC: Cataloging Distribution Service, Library of Congress). ISSN 1048–9711.

[12]*Facts on File; World News Digest with Index* (New York: Facts on File, weekly). Also available in electronic format (Dialog File 264; CD-ROM format).

[13]*The International Year Book and Statesmen's Who's Who: International and National Organizations, Countries of the Word, and 8,000 Biographies of Leading Personalities in Public Life.* East Grinstead, England: Reed Information Services, annual) ISBN 0611009307.

[14]*Merriam-Webster's Biographical Dictionary* (Springfield, MA: Merriam Webster, 1995). ISBN 0877797439.

[15]*Webster's Biographical Dictionary* (Springfield, MA: Merriam Webster, 1966).

[16]*Dictionary of American Biography* (New York: Charles Scribner's Son, 1996; Complete through supplement ten). ISBN 0684804824.

[17]Sir Leslie Stephen, and Sir Sidney Lee, eds. *Dictionary of National Biography.* (London: Smith, Elder & Co., 1908–1909; reprint).

[18]*Chamber's Biographical Dictionary,* rev. ed. (Edinburgh: Chambers, 1990). ISBN 055016040X.

[19]David Crystal, ed. *The Cambridge Biographical Encyclopedia* (Cambridge: Cambridge University Press, 1994). ISBN 0521434211.

[20]*Who's Who in the World,* 14th ed. (Wilmette, IL: Marquis Who's Who, 1997). ISBN 0837911176.

[21]Frank R. Abate, ed., *Proper Names Master Index: A Comprehensive Index of More than 200,000 Names that Appear as Entries in Standard Reference Works* (Detroit: Omnigraphics, 1994). ISBN 1558888373.

[22]OCLC is the world's largest bibliographic database and follows Library of Congress and Dewey Decimal classification schemes. FirstSearch WorldCat is the public access version of this database.

[23]*Encyclopedia of Associations: An Associations Unlimited Resource: A Guide to More than 23,000 National and International Organizations,* 32d ed. (Detroit, MI: Gale Research, Inc., 1997). ISBN 0787608459.

[24]Susan Mayhew, *A Dictionary of Geography* (New York: Oxford University Press, 1997). ISBN 0192800345.

[25]*Merriam-Webster's Geographical Dictionary,* 3d ed. (Springfield, MA: Merriam Webster, 1997). ISBN 0877795460. There is also a small, pocket-size version of this dictionary that has 12,000 entries.

[26]*Columbia-Lippincott Gazetteer of the World* (New York: Columbia University Press, 1952, with 1961 supplement).

[27]Bruce P. Lenman, *Larousse Dictionary of World History* (Edinburgh: Larousse, 1995). ISBN 0752350080 (paperback).

[28]Simon Homblower, ed., *The Oxford Classical Dictionary,* 3d ed. (New York: Oxford University Press, 1996). ISBN 019866172X.

[29]*Dictionary of British History (Lincolnwood, IL: NTC Publishing Group, 1996). ISBN 0844209279.*

[30]Robert Ferrell, ed., *Dictionary of American History* (New York: Prentice Hall International, 1996). ISBN 0684195798.

[31]*Acronyms, Initialisms, and Abbreviations Dictionary,* 22d ed. (Detroit, MI: Gale Research, 1997). ISBN 0787600369.

[32]*Reverse Acronyms, Initialisms, and Abbreviations Dictionary: A Companion Volume to Acronyms, Initialisms, and Abbreviations Dictionary with Terms Arranged Alphabetically by Meaning of Acronym, Initialism, or Abbreviation,* 22d ed., 3 vols. (Detroit, MI: Gale Research, 1997).

[33]*East Europe, Reference Aid: Abbreviations Used in the Czech and Slovak Press* (Arlington, VA: Foreign Broadcast Information Service, 1996).

[34]*International Acronyms. Initialisms, and Abbreviations Dictionary.* 3d ed. (Detroit: Gale Research, 1993). ISBN 0810374315.

[35]William R. Evinger, ed., *Guide to Federal Government Acronyms* (Phoenix: Oryx Press, 1989). ISBN 089774586.

[36] *The Dictionary of Art* (New York: Grove Dictionaries, 1996). ISBN 1884446000.

[37]*Encyclopedia of World Art,* 17 vols. (New York: McGraw-Hill, 1959–1987). ISBN 007019467X.

[38]Harold Osborne, ed. *The Oxford Companion to Art* (Oxford: Clarendon, 1989). ISBN 019866107X.

[39]Ian Chilvers, and Harold Osborne, eds. *The Oxford Dictionary of Art* (New York: Oxford University Press, 1986. ISBN 0198661339. There is also *The Concise Oxford Dictionary of Art & Artists,* a smaller version of the larger book, published in 1996 (ISBN 0192800485, paperback).

[40]James Vinson, ed., *International Dictionary of Art and Artists,* 2 vols. (Chicago: St. James Press, 1990).

[41]John A. Walker, *Glossary of Art, Architecture, and Design Since 1945,* 3d ed. (London: Library Association Publishing, 1992). ISBN 0816105561.

[42]Ralph Mayer, *The HarperCollins Dictionary of Art Terms and Techniques,* 2d ed. (New York: HarperPerennial, 1991). ISBN 0064610128 (paperback).

[43]Paul Cummings, *Dictionary of Contemporary American Artists,* 6th ed. (New York: St. Martin's Press, 1994). ISBN 0312084404.

[44]Yutaka Tazawa, *Biographical Dictionary of Japanese Art* (Tokyo: Kodansha International, 1981). ISBN 0870114883.

[45]Glenn B. Opitz, *Dictionary of American Sculptors: 18th Century to the Present* (New York: Apollo Books, 1984). ISBN 0938290037.

[46]*Medieval Art: A Topical Dictionary* (Westport, CT: Greenwood Press, 1996). ISBN 0313293295.

[47]William Rose Benet, *Benet's Reader's Encyclopedia,* 4th ed. (New York: Harper Collins Publishers, 1996). ISBN 0061810886.

[48]Wendell V. Harris, *Dictionary of Concepts in Literary Criticism* (New York: Greenwood Press, 1992). ISBN 0313259321.

[49]J. A. Cuddon, *Dictionary of Literary Terms and Theory,* 3d ed. rev. (New York: Penguin, 1992). ISBN 0140512276 (paperback).

[50]Martin Coyle, et al., eds., *Encyclopedia of Literature and Criticism* (Detroit, MI: Gale Research, 1991). ISBN 0810383314.

[51]Leonard Klein, general ed., *Encyclopedia of World Literature in the 20th Century,* 2d ed. rev., 5 vols. (New York: Ungar, 1981–1993).

[52]Matthew J. Bruccoli, et al., *Dictionary of Literary Biography* (Detroit, MI: Gale Research, 1978–). An example of a recent title from this series is *South Slavic Writers Since World War II,* vol. 181 (1997).

[53]T. J. Carty, *Dictionary of Literary Pseudonyms in the English Language* (London: Mansell, 1996). ISBN 072012221X

[54]Stanley Sadie, ed., *The New Grove Dictionary of Music and Musicians.* 20 vols. (New York: Grove's Dictionaries of Music, 1995). ISBN 1561591742 (paperback).

[55]H. Willey Hitchcock and Stanley Sadie, *The New Grove Dictionary of American Music,* 4 vols. (New York: Grove's Dictionaries of Music, 1992). ISBN 0943818362.

[56]Michael Kennedy, *The Concise Oxford Dictionary of Music* (New York: Oxford University Press, 1996). ISBN 019280037X (paperback).

[57]Perry Bratcher, et al., *Music Subject Headings: Compiled from Library of Congress Subject Headings* (Lake Crystal, MN: Soldier Creek Press, 1988). ISBN 0936996315 (paperback).

[58]Walter Kaufmann, *Selected Musical Terms of Non-Western Culture* (Warren, MI: Harmonic Park Press, 1990). ISBN 0899900399.

[59]Nicholas Slonimsky, *Thesaurus of Scales and Melodic Patterns* (New York: Macmillan, 1997). ISBN 0026118505.

[60]Horst Leuchtmann, ed., *Dictionary of Terms in Music: English-German, German-English* (Providence, NIJ K. G. Saur, 1992). ISBN 359810913X.

[61]*An Early Music Dictionary* (New York: Cambridge University Press, 1995). ISBN 0521416884.

[62]These areas are metaphysics, epistemology, logic, ethics, and aesthetics.

[63]Paul Edwards, ed., *Encyclopedia of Philosophy,* 8 vols. (New York: Macmillan, 1972).

[64]Simon Blackburn, *The Oxford Dictionary of Philosophy* (New York: Oxford University Press, 1996). ISBN 0192831348 (paperback).

[65]Thomas Mautner, *A Dictionary of Philosophy* (Cambridge, MA: Blackwell, 1996). ISBN 0631184597.

[66]*The Cambridge Dictionary of Philosophy* (Cambridge: Cambridge University Press, 1995). ISBN 052148328X.

[67]A. W Sparkes, *Talking Philosophy: A Wordbook* (New York: Routledge, 1991). ISBN 0415042232 (paperback).

[68]*Companion Encyclopedia of Asian Philosophy* (London: Routledge, 1997). ISBN 041503535X.

[69]A. J. Hastings, et al., eds., *Encyclopedia of Religion and Ethics,* 13 vols. (New York: Scribners, 1980; reprint).

[70]Richard Cavendish and Brian Innes, eds. *Man, Myth, and Magic: The Illustrated Encyclopedia of Mythology, Religion, and the Unknown,* 21 vols. (New York: Marshall Cavendish, 1997). ISBN 185435731X.

[71]*Encyclopedia of Jewish Concepts* (New York: Hebrew Publishing Co., 1993). ISBN 0884829308.

[72]*The Blackwell Dictionary of Judaica* (Oxford: Blackwell Reference, 1992). ISBN 0631187286 (paperback).

[73]*Encyclopedia Judaica,* 17 vols. (Jerusalem: Keter, 1982; reprint). ISBN 0685362531.

[74]*New Catholic Encyclopedia,* 18 vols. (Palatine, IL: Jack Heraty, 1989). ISBN 007010235. Also includes supplements.

[75]David Hugh Farmer, *The Oxford Dictionary of Saints,* 4th ed. (New York: Oxford University Press, 1997). ISBN 0192800582.

[76]J. N. D. Kelly, *The Oxford Dictionary of Popes* (New York: Oxford University Press, 1988). ISBN 0192820850 (paperback).

[77]Mustansir Mir, *Dictionary of Quranic Terms and Concepts* (New York: Garland Pub., 1987). ISBN 0824085469.

[78]Thomas Patrick Hughes, *Dictionary of Islam,* New Canadian Edition (Ottawa: Laurier Books, 1996). ISBN 18959187.

[79]H. A. R. Gibb, et al., eds., *Encyclopedia of Islam,* 5 vols. (London: Luzac, 1960— plus supplements and fascicles).

[80]*International Biographical Dictionary of Religion* (Munich: Saur, 1994). ISBN 3598111002.

[81]K. G. B. Bakewell, "Reference Books for Indexers," *The Indexer* 15 (1987): 131– 40, 195–96. This has been updated as a publication of the Society of Indexers as *Information Sources and Reference Tools,* by K. G. B. Bakewell. 2d ed. Revised by Pat F. Booth (1993). ISBN 1871577101.

[82]*Guide to Reference Books,* 11th ed. (Chicago: American Library Association, 1996). ISBN 0838906699.

[83]*ARBA Guide to Subject Encyclopedias and Dictionaries,* 2d ed. (Englewood, CO: Libraries Unlimited, 1997). ISBN 1563084678.

[84]See Blazek and Aversa, *The Humanities* (1994) and *Books for College Libraries: Humanities,* vol. 1 (Chicago: American Library Association, 1988). ISBN 0838933572.

[85]Thomas Kabdebo, *Dictionary of Dictionaries* (London: Bowker-Saur, 1992). ISBN 0862917751.

[86]Kenneth Kister, Kister's Best Encyclopedias: A Comparative Guide to General and Specialized Encyclopedias, 2d ed. (Phoenix: Oryx Press, 1994). ISBN 0897747445.

[87]*Books in Print* (New York: R. R. Bowker, annual).

Chapter 9
Social Science
Reference Works

Cynthia D. Bertelsen[*]

Indexers working with social science subjects must be familiar with a large number of disciplines unless they specialize in one area only. For the purposes of this article, the social sciences are defined as economics/business, history/geography, political science/law,[1] and sociology/anthropology. Each of these disciplines has its own manner of presenting research and theory, each has its own special terminology, and each actually merits an article of its own. Thus, the social sciences indexer; who may not always be a subject expert, often finds it necessary to refer to a number of reference materials in order to clarify any problems that arise during the indexing process. A growing problem in the social sciences is what Mattei Dogan calls "the hybridization of social science knowledge."[2]

These problems tend to be similar, of course, to the problems found in other subject areas where there is borrowing across disciplines; i.e., synonyms and cross-referencing. However, social sciences indexers tend to have more inconsistencies with names of persons, places, and corporate bodies, particularly when the volume to be indexed is a multi-authored one. Acronyms can also be quite prevalent in social sciences texts and often need to be clarified for the index user. Additional issues arise from the research methodology used in the social sciences, with their increasing emphasis on quantitative statistical analysis for data interpretation and conceptual theories.

The social sciences indexer cannot be expected to have a full-fledged research reference collection at his or her fingertips, but investing in some basic reference tools can save time in the long run and ensure crucial accuracy. The following discussion of reference tools for the social sciences indexer presents a

[*] Reprinted with permission, from *Key Words*, the newsletter of the American Society of Indexers 5, nos. 3/4 (May/June & Jul/Aug 1997): 26–29.

number of inexpensive materials (denoted by paperback versions) as well as items that will only be found in academic research libraries.

Choosing Reference Sources

To begin with, how should an indexer choose reference materials? The following criteria are guidelines[3] that are generally used by librarians in book selection:

1. Purpose and scope of the work: In other words, what does this work have to offer? What aspects of a subject does it cover? What is unique about it in comparison to others like it?
2. Authority of the author or publisher: Is this work produced by an authority in the field? Are the author's or publisher's other works well-reviewed and/or listed in bibliographies for core library collections in the subject area?
3. Currency of the material: is the material up to dare? If the work has been published for some time, is it updated regularly?
4. Format of the material: Does the format make it an easy source to use?

The following reference tools, both basic core references and those grouped by problem area, were chosen because of their currency, placement in bibliographies for core collections for academic libraries, and their usefulness to the indexer who may not always be a subject expert. Some were suggested by indexers in response to a query to indexers on INDEX-L: I asked indexers on INDEX-L to share with me their favorite or most necessary reference materials for indexing specific subject matter. (Internet sources, unless the resource is an online version of print material, are nor included here, due to questions about the authority of the compiler in some cases and accuracy of the information included in various World Wide Web sites.)

Core Resources

Many indexing problems faced by the social sciences indexer can be remedied with what might best be called a core reference collection. Materials in this collection include tools to deal with acronyms, names of well-known people both living and dead, and basic terminology for the social sciences as a whole. One of the most basic, and inexpensive, tools is *The World Almanac and Book of Facts*,[4] published annually and therefore valuable for its currency. Names of politicians and celebrities, information on American history and geography, as well as descriptions of foreign nations are included. *The International Encyclopedia of the Social Sciences*[5] is another general work which includes a broad range of discussions of various aspects of the social sciences; somewhat our of date, the work still has merit in its comprehensiveness and the fact that it was edited by a number of editors from 30 countries, including non-Western countries.

Dictionaries of ideas are another source for the indexer who is not a subject expert. Two of the most recently published of these works is *The Hutchinson Dictionary of Ideas*[6] and *Dictionary of Theories,*[7] with a broad range of entries on a number of major concepts in human knowledge. Of course, the legendary *Encyclopedia Britannica* should be part of the indexer's reference library, because of its major subject outline discussion articles as well as shorter entries on most of humankind's knowledge. The online version is particularly useful because of its search capabilities, which saves time for the busy indexer.[8] The *Library of Congress Subject Headings (LCSH),*[9] while definitely limited in some of their more politically incorrect usages, do provide cross-referencing guidelines for terms.

Names, Organizations, and Places

Biographical dictionaries that list names of persons no longer living include *Webster's New Biographical Dictionary,*[10] *Webster's Biographical Dictionary,*[11] *Dictionary of American Biography,*[12] and *Dictionary of National Biography.*[13] For names of living persons, use *Webster's New Biographical Dictionary, Chamber's Biographical Dictionary,*[14] *The Cambridge Biographical Encyclopedia,*[15] and the *Who's Who* series by Marquis.[16] Many countries also publish their own Who's Who volumes as well; see, for example, *Bowker-Saur's Who's Who in European Business.*[17]

Verification of names, and especially name order, is a continual problem for the social sciences indexer, especially when the text covers non-Western societies or languages that are not written originally in Roman script. Consulting various country-specific dictionaries is necessary in these cases, but if the name in question is of a person, place, or organization that is in the current news, *Facts on File: World News Digest* is a possible source,[18] as is *The International Year Book and Statesmen's Who's Who: International and National Organizations, Countries of the World, and 5,000 Biographies of Leading Personalities in Public Life.*[19] Finally, if a person has been written about or has written a book, the Library of Congress Authority File will have information about the correct form of the name and this is to be found in library catalogs or OCLC's FirstSearch Service catalog, WorldCat.[20]

Apart from names of persons, names of organizations also present trying problems at times for the indexer. A helpful reference for verification of names of organizations is the *Encyclopedia of Associations: An Associations Unlimited Resource: A Guide to More than 23,000 National and International Organizations.*[21] *Brands and Their Companies*[22] and *Companies and Their Brands*[23] are two other complementary works that are useful for verification of company names and affiliates.

Geographical names sometimes must be identified in indexes, and Oxford University Press' new edition of the *Mayhew* dictionary contains up-to-date information on the changes that occurred after the break-up of the Soviet Union.[24] Other favorites, though dated, are *Merriam-Webster's Geographical Dictionary*[25] and the *Columbia-Lippincott Gazetteer of the World,* good for historical reference.[26] Area-specific historical and political atlases are also available.

Acronyms

Acronyms present another problem in social sciences indexing. In many cases, authors assume that the reader knows the meaning of the acronym, which may not be the case at all. Hence, it is up to the indexer to provide this information by using dictionaries of acronyms. One of the best sources for this problem is Gale Research's *Acronyms, Initialisms, and Abbreviations Dictionary*[27] and its companion volume, *Reverse Acronyms, Initialisms, and Abbreviations Dictionary: A Companion Volume to Acronyms, Initialisms, and Abbreviations Dictionary with Terms Arranged Alphabetically by Meaning of Acronym, Initialism, or Abbreviation.*[28] For international acronyms, the Foreign Broadcast Information Service[29] has published a series of works on acronyms used in the press and media of certain geographical areas, including the Third World. U.S. government agencies, notorious for their acronyms, can be determined by the use of the slightly outdated *Guide to Federal Government Acronyms.*[30]

Synonyms and Concepts

Acronyms and names aside, very possibly the biggest issue for the social sciences indexer is the inclusion of synonyms and other suitable cross-referencing terms to fully capture the concepts discussed in a text. The nature of social sciences research and its broad spectrum demands that indexes be as comprehensive as possible in terms of conceptual terminology. This terminology may not always be referred to by the author, but readers may be looking for it. An example of this situation is to be found in statistics as it relates to sociological studies: a probability sample and a random sample are the same thing. A cross-reference from probability sample to random sample might be in order; likewise, a heading of sampling might be referred to as well. General tools such as thesauri like *The Contemporary Thesaurus of Social Science Terms and Synonyms: A Guide for Natural Language Computer Searching*[31] and *Thesaurus of Sociological Indexing Terms*[32] are useful, as are the more outdated *A Dictionary of Social Science Methods*[33] and *Dictionary of Statistics and Methodology: A Nontechnical Guide for the Social Sciences.*[34] UNESCO's series of thematic descriptors may also be of help at times.[34]

Subject-specific works become extremely important for the indexer when ideas and concepts are not well defined by the author or when the indexer is not a subject specialist and needs to have help with cross-referencing. Greenwood Press published several discipline-specific concept books in the 1980s and early 1990s, which are still valuable works. In short essays, each book's entries explain the major concepts of the discipline.[36] Other concept books include *Key Business Concepts: A Concise Guide,*[37] *The Illustrated Dictionary of Constitutional Concepts,*[38] and subject-specific dictionaries. The *PAlS Subject Headings*[39] is a particularly useful source for terms since it contains *See* and *See also* alternate terms.

Subject-specific dictionaries abound; there is even one entitled *Dictionary of Old Trades and Occupations,* which may be of interest to the indexer of certain historical works.[40] As any indexer knows, no subject is too esoteric for it to be the theme of a book. However, the major concern is to have on hand a easy-to-use, reliable source for common issues that arise during the indexing process.

Indexers of sociology and anthropological texts will want to look at *The HarperCollins Dictionary of Sociology*[41] (with 1,800 entries, is a concise and inexpensive dictionary of help in indexing sociological texts) and Blackwell's *The Dictionary of Anthropology.*[42] Indexing of historical and political science works is enhanced by the *Larousse Dictionary of World History,*[43] the Scarecrow Press' *Historical Dictionaries* series like the one for Togo (these are also excellent for name verification problems),[44] the ABC-Clio dictionaries in political series, like the ones for the Middle East and international relations,[45] and political science dictionaries like *The Concise Oxford Dictionary of Politics.*[46]Most periods of history have their own dictionaries, such as *The Oxford Classical Dictionary.*[47] Countries also have specific historical dictionaries;

see, for example, the *Dictionary of British History*[48] and the two-volume *Dictionary of American History*.[49] Legal indexers rely on *Black's Law Dictionary*[50] and the *Legal Thesaurus*,[51] while economics terms can be verified with the *Routledge Dictionary of Economics*[52] and *Business Thesaurus*.[53]

How to Find What You Need

If the materials listed here do not answer a specific question that arises, finding what you need when it comes to a specific indexing problem in a specific subject area is not always easy. K. G. B. Bakewell wrote a helpful article on basic references for indexers, since revised, which points out reference tools that aid indexers in the indexing process. The materials are arranged by type of material; i.e., directories, encyclopedias, and the like.[54] However, perhaps the easiest way to find a particular reference book is to ask your local librarian or to take a look at standard bibliographies of reference books, such as the American Library Association's latest issue of *Guide to Reference Books*[55] and the *ARBA (American Reference Books Annual) Guide to Subject Encyclopedias and Dictionaries*.[56] Doing an online search of FirstSearch can be fruitful or fruitless, depending on what terms you use in the search. (See note 18). *Books in Print*[57] provides information on books currently in print.

Summing Up

Indexers have a number of problems to deal with while indexing social sciences texts. Name verification for persons, organizations, and places are among those problems, as are problems with acronyms. Term selection and cross-referencing of concepts are the most important issues facing the social sciences indexer, who has a wide variety of general and subject-specific reference tools to which to turn. Although the terminology of the author is always the first choice of the indexer, it is often necessary to create cross-references to and from the author's terms to others that might occur to the index user. This is where is behooves the indexer to have a good idea of where those terms are defined, if the author doesn't provide that information.

Notes

[1]For an in-depth discussion of legal indexing and its appropriate references, see Elizabeth M. Moys, et al. eds., *Indexing Legal Materials*, Occasional Papers on Indexing, no.2. (London: Society of Indexers, 1993).

[2]Mattei Dogan, "The Hybridization of Social Science Knowledge," *Library Trends* 45/2 (1996): 296–314. See also Robert Pahre, "Patterns of Knowledge Communities in the Social Sciences" *Library Trends* 45/2 (1996): 204–25.

[3]William A. Katz, *Introduction to Reference Work,* 6th ed., vol. 1 (New York: McGraw-Hill, 1992), 24–29.

[4]*The World Almanac and Book of Facts* (annual) (Mahwah, NJ: World Almanac Books). ISBN 0886878004 (paperback).

[5]*International Encyclopedia of the Social Sciences* (New York: Macmillan, 1968–1991). ISBN 002897395X.

[6]*The Hutchinson Dictionary of Ideas* (Oxford: Helicon, 1995). ISBN 1859860508 (paperback).

[7]*Dictionary of Theories,* ed. Jennifer Bothamley (Detroit, MI: Gale Research, 1993).

[8]Access *Encyclopedia Britannica* through http://www.eb.com. There is a free trial period, and then an inexpensive monthly fee after that.

[9]*Library of Congress Subject Headings.* 19th ed. 4 vols. Washington, DC: Cataloging Distribution Service, Library of Congress. ISSN 1048–9711.

[10]*Merriam-Webster's New Biographical Dictionary* (Springfield, MA: Merriam Webster, 1995). ISBN 0877797439.

[11]*Webster's Biographical Dictionary* (Springfield, MA: Merriam Webster, 1966–).

[12]*Dictionary of American Biography* (New York: Scribners, 1996–). ISBN 0684804824.

[13]*Dictionary of National Biography: From the Earliest Times through 1900*, ed. Leslie Stephen and Sidney Lee (London: Smith, Elder & Co., 1908–1909, reprint; supplements through 1930).

[14]*Chamber's Biographical Dictionary,* Rev. ed. (Edinburgh: Chambers, 1990). ISBN 055016040X

[15]*The Cambridge Biographical Encyclopedia,* ed. David Crystal (Cambridge: Cambridge University Press, 1994). ISBN 0521434211.

[16]*Who's Who in the World,* etc. (Wilmette, IL: Marquis Who's Who, biannual)

[17]*Who's Who in European Business* (New York: Bowker–Saur, 1993–). Serial. ISBN 0862917956.

[18]*Facts on File: World News Digest with Index* (New York: Facts on File, weekly). ISBN, Electronic format (Dialog File 264; CD–ROM format also)

[19]*The International Year Book and Statesmen's Who's Who: International and National Organizations Countries of the World, and 8,000 Biographies of Leading Personalities in Public Life* (E. Grinstead, Eng.: Reed Information Services, 1996, annual). ISBN 0611009307.

[20]OCLC is the world's largest bibliographic database and follows Library of Congress and Dewey Decimal classification schemes. FirstSearch WorldCat is a public access version of this database.

[21]*Encyclopedia of Associations: An Associations Unlimited Resource: A Guide to More than 23,000 National and International Organizations,* 32nd ed. (Detroit, MI: Gale Research, 1997). ISBN 0787608459.

[22]*Brands and Their Companies* (Detroit, MI: Gale Research, annual). ISBN 0787609854.

[23]*Companies and Their Brands* (Detroit, MI: Gale Research, annual). ISBN 0810302136.

[24]*A Dictionary of Geography,* ed. Susan May (New York: Oxford University Press, 1997). ISBN 0192800345.

[25]*Merriam–Webster's Geographical Dictionary* (Springfield, MA: Merriam-Webster, 1988). ISBN 0877795460. (There is also a pocket–size version of this dictionary that has 12,000 entries.)

[26]*Columbia-Lippincott Gazetteer of the World* (New York: Columbia University Press, 1952, with 1961 supplement)

[27]*Acronyms, Initialisms, and Abbreviations Dictionary,* 22d ed. (Detroit, MI: Gale Research, 1997). ISBN 0787600369.

[28]*Reverse Acronyms, Initialisms, and Abbreviations Dictionary: A Companion Volume to Acronyms, Initialisms, and Abbreviations Dictionary with Terms Arranged Alphabetically by Meaning of Acronym, Initialism, or Abbreviation,* 22nd ed., 3 vols. (Detroit, MI: Gale Research, 1997).

[29]*East Europe, Reference Aid: Abbreviations Used in the Czech and Slovak Press* (Arlington, VA: Foreign Broadcast Information Service, 1996).

[30]*Guide to Federal Government Acronyms,* ed. William R. Evinger (Phoenix, AZ: Oryx Press, 1989). ISBN 089774586.

[31]*The Contemporary Thesaurus of Social Science Terms and Synonyms: A Guide for Natural Language Computer Searching,* Sara D. Knapp (Phoenix, AZ: Oryx Press, 1993). ISBN 0897745957.

[32]*Thesaurus of Sociological Indexing Terms,* 3rd ed., Barbara Booth (San Diego: Sociological Abstracts, 1992). ISBN 0930710134.

[33]*A Dictionary of Social Science Methods,* P. McC. Miller (New York: Wiley, 1984).

[34]*Dictionary of Statistics and Methodology: A Nontechnical Guide for the Social Sciences,* Paul W. Vogt (Newbury Park, CA: Sage Publications, 1993). ISBN 0803952775 (paperback).

[35]*Thematic List of Descriptors—Anthropology.* UNESCO (New York: Routledge, 1989). ISBN 0415017769. *Thematic List of Descriptors—Political Science.* UNESCO. (New York: Routledge, 1989). ISBN 0415017785. *Thematic List of Descriptor—Sociology.* UNESCO (New York: Routledge, 1989). ISBN 0415017793.

[36]*Dictionary of Concepts in Cultural Anthropology,* Robert H. Winthrop (Westport, CT: Greenwood Press, 1991). ISBN 0313242801. *Dictionary of Concepts in History* Harry Ritter, (London: Greenwood/Eurospan, 1987). ISBN 0313227004. *Dictionary of Concepts in Human Geography,* Robert P. Larkin (Westport, CT: Greenwood Press, 1983). ISBN 0313227292. *Dictionary of Concepts in Physical Anthropology,* Joan C. Stevenson (Westport, CT: Greenwood Press, 1991). ISBN 0313247560.

[37]*Key Business Concepts: A Concise Guide,* Bengt Karlof (New York: Routledge, 1993). ISBN 0415088534.

[38]*The Illustrated Dictionary of Constitutional Concepts,* Robert L. Maddex (Washington, DC, Congressional Quarterly1996). ISBN 1568021704.

[39]*PAIS Subject Headings,* 2d ed. (New York: Public Affairs Information Service, 1990). ISBN 1877874019.

[40]*Dictionary of Old Trades and Occupations,* 2nd ed., Andrew Twining (Woodcroft, S. Australia, Twining's Secretarial, 1995). ISBN 0646257129.

[41]*The HarperCollins Dictionary of Sociology,* ed. Julia Jary and David Jary (New York: Harper Perennial, 1991). ISBN 0064610365 (paperback).

[42]*The Dictionary of Anthropology* (Cambridge, MA: Blackwell, 1997). ISBN 157862826.

[43]*Larousse Dictionary of World History,* Bruce P. Lenman (Edinburgh: Larousse plc, 1995). ISBN 0752350080 (paperback).

[44]*Historical Dictionary of Togo,* Samuel Decalo (Metuchen, NJ: Scarecrow Press, 1996). ISBN 0810830736.

[45]*International Relations: A Political Dictionary,* ed. Lawrence Ziring (Santa Barbara, CA: ABC–Clio, 1995). ISBN 0874368979. *The Middle East: A Political Dictionary,* Lawrence Ziring (Santa Barbara, CA: ABC–Clio, 1992). ISBN 0874366976.

[46]*The Concise Oxford Dictionary of Politics* (New York: Oxford University Press, 1996). ISBN 0192852884 (paperback).

[47]*The Oxford Classical Dictionary,* 3d ed., ed. Simon Hornblower (New York: Oxford University Press, 1996). ISBN 019866172X

[48]*Dictionary of British History* (Lincolnwood, IL: NTC Publishing Group, 1996). ISBN 0844209279.

[49]*Dictionary of American History,* ed. Robert Ferrell (New York: Charles Scribner's Sons Reference Books: Prentice Hall International, 1996). ISBN 0684195798.

[50]*Black's Law Dictionary,* 6th ed. Henry Campbell Black (St. Paul, MN: West Publ. Co., 1990). ISBN 031476271X.

[51]*Legal Thesaurus,* 2d ed., William C. Burton (New York: Macmillan, 1992). ISBN 0028970799 (paperback).

[52]*Routledge Dictionary of Economics,* Donald Rutherford (New York: Routledge, 1995). ISBN 0415122910.

[53]*Business Thesaurus,* Mary A. Devries (New York: Barrons Educational Series, 1996). ISBN 0812093275 (paperback).

[54]K.G.B. Bakewell, "Reference Books for Indexers," *The Indexer* 15 (1987): 131–40, 195–96. This has been updated as *Information Sources and Reference Tools,* by K. G. B. Bakewell, 2d ed., revised by Pat F. Booth (Society of Indexers, 1993). ISBN 1871577101.

[55]*Guide to Reference Books,* 11th ed. Chicago: American Library Association, 1966). ISBN 0838906699.

[56]*ARBA Guide to Reference Books,* 2d ed. (Englewood, CO: Libraries Unlimited, 1997). ISBN 1563084678.

[57]*Books in Print* (New York: R. R. Bowker, annual).

Chapter 10
Medical Reference Works

Cynthia D. Bertelsen[*]

Medical indexers have a very important obligation to the index users of the materials they index (usually physicians, nurses, and other health professionals as well as lay readers) and to the people (usually patients) who are helped by those index users. Poorly or inaccurately indexed material could, in the wrong situation, mean serious injury, unnecessary suffering, or even death for someone.

The importance of the right medical reference tools, therefore, cannot be stressed too much. Generally, the terminology of the author is preferred, but in cases involving term inconsistencies in multi-authored texts or other similar problems, the indexer must pay special attention to term selection. Common problems for the medical indexer include the following: term selection, spelling of terms, use of synonyms and eponyms, drug names, names of organizations and agencies, names of medical experts, and abbreviations. While the medical indexer cannot be expected to have a full-fledged reference library on hand, an investment in some reference tools can save time in the long run and ensure crucial accuracy. Other, more expensive reference sources are often available at local libraries.

Choosing Reference Sources

How should an indexer chose reference materials? The following criteria are guidelines generally used by librarians for book selection.[1]

1. Purpose and scope of the work: in other words, what does this work have to offer? What aspects of a subject does it cover? What is unique about it in comparison to others like it?
2. Authority of the author or publisher: Is this work produced by an authority in the field? Are the author's or publisher's other works

---

[*] Reprinted with permission, from *Key Words*, the newsletter of the American Society of Indexers 5, no. 1 (Jan/Feb 1997): 7–9.

3. well-reviewed and/or listed in bibliographies for core library collections in the subject area?
3. Currency of the material: Is the material up to date? If the work has been published for some time, is it updated regularly?
4. Format of the material: Does the format make it an easy source to use?

The following reference tools, grouped by type of medical indexing problem, were chosen because of their currency, placement in bibliographies for core collections for medical libraries, and their usefulness to the medical indexer.

Many of the tools were mentioned by indexers at the 1996 ASI meeting in Denver. Others were suggested by indexers in response to a query on INDEX-L: I asked indexers on INDEX-L to share with me their favorite or most necessary reference materials for indexing specific subject matter. (Internet sources, unless the resource is an on-line version of print material, are not included here because of questions about the authority of the compiler in some cases and accuracy of the information included at various World Wide Web sites.)

Term Selection

SPELLING. The spelling of medical terms can be a problem, because a word may be misspelled in the text itself, one author may use a British variant of the term and another the American, or an author may create a new term altogether by using Greek and Latin prefixes and suffixes. A good medical dictionary such as *Garlands, Black's, Stedman's,* or *Churchill's* is mandatory (see nn. 5–8). Other reference tools include computerized medical spellcheckers or dictionaries, such as the one produced by Indexing Research (producers of Cindex) or *Stedman's*[2] on disk which can be added to a dedicated indexing software program or to a word processing program.

MeSH. Carolyn Weaver, a medical librarian and indexer at the University of Washington,[3] stated that the Medical Subject Headings (MeSH)[4] is the basic tool that she uses for term selection. Published by the National Library of Medicine (NLM), MeSH has merits in that it serves as "an aid in identifying potential index terms/synonyms/cross-refs.... In multi-authored works or a journal index where several synonyms are used for the same concept, I often use the MeSH term as the entry point, with cross-references from other terms." MeSH's particular value lies not only in its help with synonym selection, but it also provides an almost universal controlled vocabulary, albeit with American spellings. Nevertheless, MeSH is a valuable tool for the medical indexer. It is updated annually.

Synonyms and Eponyms

Another problem for the medical indexer is the presence in medical literature of many synonymous terms. Eponyms, for example, are an interesting facet of medical indexing, along the same lines as biological nomenclature of species where a form of the discoverer's name is part of the species name. In the case of eponyms, the name of the person who either first described the disease or otherwise is associated with the disease or condition is included in the name; i.e., Alzheimer's (presenile dementia) or Stanton's disease (melioidosis). Cross-references must be made from eponyms and synonyms to one main heading for the disease.

Tools that assist the indexer in the selection of synonymous terms include:

MEDICAL DICTIONARIES. For example, *Black's Medical Dictionary*,[5] *Churchill's Illustrated Medical Dictionary*,[6] Dorland's *Illustrated Medical Dictionary*,[7] *Stedman's Medical Dictionary*[8]; nearly all have various synonyms included in descriptions of diseases and conditions.

DICTIONARIES OF SYNONYMS AND EPONYMS. The *Dictionary of Medical Eponyms*,[9] *Jablonski's Dictionary of Syndromes & Eponymic Diseases*.[10]

MEDICAL WORD FINDERS. The lay term is associated with the correct medical term or terms: *Medical Word Finder: A Reverse Medical Dictionary*,[11] *Webster's New World Medical Word Finder*.[12] *Jablonski's Dictionary*, in particular, was mentioned at the 1996 ASI conference in Denver as an excellent resource.

Abbreviations and Acronyms

Because acronyms and abbreviations, like CAT scan or CT scan, are an important part of medical terminology, a dictionary like Dupayrat's *Dictionary of Biomedical Acronyms and Abbreviations*[13] or others such as *Dictionary of Medical Acronyms & Abbreviations*,[14] *Logan's Medical and Scientific Abbreviations*[15] are extremely useful. The acronym or abbreviation is defined and spelled out in full, giving the indexer a cross-reference to or from the acronym. Because medicine is international in scope and daily becoming more so, the *Dictionary of International Medical Abbreviations*[16] is an important reference as well.

Drug Names and Other Pharmacological Nightmares

Drug names are among the most difficult to index, because there are generic names, proprietary or brand names, chemical names, popular names, and names common in other countries. No one resource can answer all of these problems, but some of the more helpful resources include the yearly *Physicians' Desk Reference (PDR)*[17] *Pharmacology Field Reference Guide,*[18] and the *Merck Manual.*[19] Mosby is publishing a new serial entitled *Mosby's 1997 Medical Drug Reference.*[20] Another comprehensive source is the *American Drug Index,*[21] also a serial, with coverage of over 20,000 drugs and references to and from chemical and brand names.

Organizations, Agencies, and People

In many cases, an indexer must verify names of people, organizations, and agencies. Using acronym and abbreviation dictionaries can help with this task (see nn. 11–14). In addition, there are directories, such as the *Encyclopedia of Medical Organizations and Agencies*[22] and the *Encyclopedia of Associations.*[23] Names of people can be located via the *Directory of Medical Specialists,*[24] with over 400,000 specialists listed; the *American Medical Directory,*[25] which lists registered physicians in the United States; the *International Medical Who's Who,*[26] listing 12,000 specialists from different countries; and the *Medical Directory,*[27] with listings for physicians in Great Britain.

Subject Dictionaries and Other Resources

Basic medical indexing problems can also be addressed with the help of various subject dictionaries and other reference tools. In particular, the field of nursing has several helpful dictionaries, with the Oxford publication, *A Dictionary of Nursing*[28] being of particular note, as does psychology.[29] Nutrition is another medically-related field that has generated several specialized reference tools.[30] For verifying laboratory tests covered in a text, there is the *Laboratory Test Handbook with Key Word Index.*[31] In addition, Williams & Wilkins publishes a line of outstanding medical reference resources too numerous to list here.

Forthcoming Resources

Publishers continue to bring out new resources and new editions of old resources of interest to indexers: *Dictionary of Medical Syndromes,*[32] *Nutrition: A Reference Handbook,*[33] and *Taber's Cyclopedic Medical Dictionary.*[34] *Publishers' Weekly,*[35] *Choice,*[36] and *Forthcoming Books*[37] are some of the resources that keep indexers current on medical reference books. The journal *Medical Reference Services Quarterly*[38] also provides information on medical reference books, as does *Medical and Health Care Books* and *Serials in Print.*[39]

Summing Up

Medical indexers generally are able to use the terminology of the author. But for fine-tuning the index and inserting appropriate synonyms and other quality markers, the medical indexer has a large number of resources available to help in solving the problems of term selection in medical indexing.

For more information on medical indexing, see *Indexing the Medical and Biological Sciences,*[40] a publication of the Society of Indexers. K. G. B. Bakewell also produced a now somewhat outdated but basically sound comprehensive list of general reference resources for indexers.[41]

Notes

[1]William A. Katz, *Introduction to Reference Work,* 6th ed., vol.1 (New York: McGraw-Hill. 1992), 24–29.

[2]*Stedman's/25 +plus for MicroSoft Word,* version 1.1 A (Baltimore: Williams & Wilkins Electronic Media, 1993) (Machine-readable format of 25th edition of *Stedman's Medical Dictionary.)*

[3]Carolyn Weaver, personal communication, INDEX-L, August 8, 1996.

[4]Medical Subject Headings (MeSH) Tree Structures; Annotated Alphabetic Lists; Permuted Medical Subject Headings NLM (1997). Order numbers (respectively): PB97–964901/LL; PB97–964801/LL; PB97–965101/LL. Send orders to: NTIS 5285 Port Royal Road, Springfield, VA 22161. Phone: 703–487–4650, Fax: 703–321–8547, Email: orders@ntis.fedworld.gov

[5]*Black's Medical Dictionary* (Cranbury, NJ: Barnes & Noble Books Imports, 1992). ISBN 0–3892–0989–9.

[6]*Churchill's Illustrated Medical Dictionary* (New York: Churchill Livingstone, 1989). ISBN 0–4430–86901–5.

[7]*Dorland's Illustrated Medical Dictionary,* 28th ed. (Philadelphia: W. B. Saunders, 1994). ISBN 0–7216–5577–7.

[8]*Stedman's Medical Dictionary,* 26th ed., (Baltimore: Williams & Wilkins, 1995). ISBN 0–6830–0722–0; 0–6830–7935–2 (deluxe ed.). This also comes in a version for WordPerfect® for both IBM and Mac. See also n. 2.

[9]*Dictionary of Medical Eponyms,* 2d ed., ed. G. B. Firkin (Pearl River: Parthenon Publishing, 1996). ISBN 1–8507–0477–5.

[10]*Jablonski's Dictionary of Syndromes & Eponymic Diseases,* ed. Stanley Jablonski (Melbourne: Krieger Publishing, 1991). ISBN 0–8946–4224–3

[11]*Medical Word Finder: A Reverse Medical Dictionary,* ed. Betty Hamilton Barbara Guidos (New York: Neal-Schuman, 1987). ISBN 1–5557–0011–X.

[12]*Webster's New World Medical Word Finder,* comp. George Willeford, Jr., (Englewood Cliffs, NJ: Prentice Hall, 1987). ISBN 0–1394–7326–2.

[13]*Dictionary of Biomedical Acnonyms & Abbreviations,* 2d ed., ed. Jacques Dupayrat, (New York: John Wiley & Sons, 1990). ISBN 0–4719–2649–3.

· [14]*Dictionary of Medical Acronyms & Abbreviations,* ed. Stanley Jablonski (Philadelphia: Hanley & Belfus, 1992). ISB N: 1–5605–3052–9.

[15]*Logan's Medical and Scientific Abbreviations,* Carolyn M. Logan, and M. Kaffierie Rice (Philadelphia: Lippincott, 1987). ISBN 0–397–54589–4.

[16]*Dictionary of International Medical Abbreviations,* ed. M. A. Touati, (New York: French & European Publications, 1994). ISBN 0–7859–8755–X.

[17]*Physician's Desk Reference* [PDR] (Oradell, NJ: Medical Economics, 1997).

[18]Richard K. Beck, *Pharmacology Field Reference Guide* (Philadelphia: F. A. Davis, 19—). ISBN 0–8036–0133–6 (paperback).

[19]*Merck Manual of Diagnosis & Therapy.* 16th ed., ed. Robert Berkow (Rahway: Merck & Co., 1992). 1SBN:0–9119–1016–6. The 1992 *Merck Manual* is available online at: http://www.merck.com/ pubs/mmanual.

[20]*Mosby's 1997 Medical Drug Reference* [serial] (St. Louis: Mosby, 1997–). ISSN 0–8151–3109–7.

[21]*American Drug Index* (St. Louis: Facts and Comparisons, 1950–). ISSN 0065–8111.

[22]*Encyclopedia of Medical Organizations and Agencies,* 4th ed., ed. Karen Backus (Detroit: Gale Research, 1992). ISBN 0–8103–6910–9 [serial].

[23]*Encyclopedia of Associations* [annual] (Detroit: Gale Research, 1956–). ISSN 0071–0202.

[24]*Directory of Medical Specialists* (Chicago: Marquis Who's Who, irregular). ISSN 0070–5829.

[25]*American Medical Directory Press of the American Medical Association* (Chicago, irregular). ISSN 0065–9339.

[26]*Medical Sciences International Who's Who,* 6th ed. (Harlow: Longman, 1994). ISBN 0–5822–5664–X.

[27]*Medical Directory* (Detroit: Gale Research, annual). ISSN 0305–3342.

[28]*A Dictionary of Nursing,* 2d ed., rev. and updated (New York: Oxford University Press, 1994). ISBN 0–1928–0027–2.

[29]*Psychiatric Dictionary,* 7th ed., ed. Robert J. Campbell (New York: Oxford University Press, 19—). ISBN 0–1951–0259–2. *The Thesaurus of Psychological Index Terms* (Washington, DC: American Psychological Association, 1994). ISBN 1–5579–8225–2.

[30]*A Dictionary of Food and Nutrition* (New York: Oxford University Press, 1995). ISBN 0–1428–8006–X. *Dictionary of Nutrition and Dietetics* (New York: Van Nostrand Reinhold, 1996). ISBN 0–1928–0006–X

[31]*Laboratory Test Handbook with Key Word Index,* David S. Jacobs (Baltimore: Williams & Wilkins, 1990). ISBN 0–683–04368–4.

[32]*Dictionary of Medical Syndromes,* 4th ed. (Philadelphia: Lippincott-Raven, 1997). ISBN 0–3975–8418–035.

[33]*Nutrition: A Reference Handbook,* ed. David A. Bender, (New York: Oxford University Press, 1997). ISBN 0–1926–2368–0.

[34]*Taber's Cyclopedic Medical Dictionary,* 18th ed., ed. Thomas L. Clayton (Philadelphia, F. A. Davis, 1997). ISBN 0–8036–0195–6.

[35]*Publishers' Weekly, The Book Industry Journal* (New York: R. R. Bowker, 1873–). ISSN 0000–0019.

[36]*Choice* (Middletown, CT: Association of College and Research Libraries, 1964). ISSN 0009–4978 [11 issues per year].

[37]*Forthcoming Books* (New York: R. R. Bowker, 1966–). ISSN 0015–8119 [bimonthly].

[38]*Medical Reference Services Quarterly* New York: Haworth Press, 1982). ISSN 0276–3869.

[39]*Medical and Health Care Books and Serials in Print* (New York: R. R. Bowker, 1971–). ISSN 0000–085X [annual].

[40]Doreen Blake, et al., *Indexing the Medical and Biological Sciences,* Occasional Papers on Indexing, no. 3 (London: Society of Indexers, 1995). ISBN 187 1577 152

[41]K. G. B. Bakewell, "Reference Books for Indexers," *The Indexer* 15 (1987):131–40, 195–96.

Chapter II
Science and Technology
Reference Works

Cynthia D. Bertelsen[*]

Indexers working with science and technology subjects must be familiar with a large number of disciplines unless they specialize in one area only. For the purposes of this article, science and technology are defined as the physical and life sciences (agriculture, astronomy, biology and zoology, chemistry, mathematics, and physics), engineering, and computer science. Each of these disciplines has its own manner of presenting research and theory, and each has its own special terminology and merits an article of its own. Thus, the indexer of science and technology subjects, who may not always be a subject expert, often finds it necessary to refer to a number of reference materials in order to clarify a number of problems that arise during the indexing process. The problems in indexing science and technology disciplines are that the pace of knowledge acquisition is becoming ever more rapid, terminology changes or is created, and disciplines merge into each other (biophysics, biotechnology, etc.).

These problems tend to be similar, of course, to the problems found in other subject areas, especially where there is borrowing across disciplines; e.g., synonyms and cross-referencing jumping back and forth from one discipline to another. Acronyms can also be quite prevalent in science and technology texts and often need to be clarified for the index user. Scientific (binomial) names or taxonomy, chemical names, symbols, and researchers' names are important components of the scientific index. Multiple-author works are common and usually contain a number of inconsistencies in terminology. In these cases the indexer must be able to narrow down multiple similar terms to a single acceptable heading. Additional issues arise from the research methodology used in the sciences and technology, with the emphasis on the visual display of quantitative statistical analysis for data interpretation and conceptual theories.

---

[*] Reprinted with permission, from *Key Words*, the newsletter of the American Society of Indexers 5, nos. 3-4 (May/Jun & Jul/Aug 1997): 30–33.

The indexer of science and technology materials cannot be expected to have a full-fledged research reference collection at his or her fingertips, but investing in some basic reference tools can save time in the long run and ensure crucial accuracy. The following discussion of reference tools for the science and technology indexer presents a number of inexpensive materials (denoted by paperback versions), as well as items that will only be found in academic research libraries, for use in solving many indexing problems.

Choosing Reference Sources

How should an indexer choose reference materials? The following criteria are guidelines that are generally used by librarians in book selection:

1. Purpose and scope of the work: What does this work have to offer? What aspects of a subject does it cover? What is unique about it in comparison to others like it?
2. Authority of the author or publisher: is this work produced by an authority in the field? Are the author's or publisher's other works well-reviewed and/or listed in bibliographies for core library collections in the subject area?
3. Currency of the material: is the material up-to-date? If the work has been published for some time, is it updated regularly?
4. Format of the material: Does the format make it an easy source to use?[1]

Following these guidelines, and keeping in mind that indexers frequently work outside their given subject specialties, the following reference tools were chosen. Included also are titles for favorite or necessary reference materials for specific subject matter that were recommended by indexers on INDEX-L. Internet materials are not included here unless they are on-line versions of print materials. In some cases, the authority of compilers and the accuracy of information on the World Wide Web can be questionable.

Core Resources

Many indexing problems faced by the science and technology indexer can be remedied with a core reference collection. Materials in this collection include tools to deal with acronyms, names of well-known scientists both living and dead, and basic terminology for the sciences as a whole. *The Larousse Dictionary of Science and Technology*[2] contains over 49,000 entries from a wide number of scientific fields. Each term is followed in parentheses by the name of the discipline in which it is used. There are a number of useful appendixes, including taxonomic classification charts. For verifying style and usage, the Council of Biological Editors' *Scientific Style and Format*[3] is also necessary. The classic *McGraw-Hill Encyclopedia of Science and Technology*[4] has recently been reissued; this 20 volume set is generally available only in libraries due to its cost but provides detailed information for a wide range of users. General references include the out-of-print *The Barnes and Noble Thesaurus of Science: All Fields of Scientific Language Explained and Illustrated*[5] (available in some libraries); *Thesaurus of Scientific, Technical, and Engineering Terms*[6] (smaller than the *McGraw-Hill Dictionary of Scientific and Technical Terms*[7] which has 105,100 terms); and the *Dictionary of Scientific Units: Including Dimensions in Numbers and Scales,*[8] useful for clarifying which scientific units are related. Other useful general references with a more specific focus include the *Dictionary of the Physical Sciences: Terms, Formulas, Data*[9] and the *Dictionary of Concepts in Philosophy of Science.*[10]

The legendary *Encyclopedia Britannica*[11] should also be part of the indexer's reference library, because of its major subject outline discussion articles, as well as shorter entries on most of humankind's knowledge. The on-line version is particularly useful because of its search capabilities, which saves time for the busy indexer. *The Library of Congress Subject Headings (LCSH),*[12] while definitely limited in some of their more politically incorrect usages, do provide general cross-referencing guidelines for terms.

Names and Organizations

Verification of names, and especially name order, is a constant problem for the science indexer, especially when the text covers non-Western societies and languages that are not written originally in Roman script. The full form of the names of scientists and researchers often need to be verified. Biographical dictionaries and directories are particularly useful for name verification problems.

General biographical dictionaries listing names of persons no longer living include *Merriam-Webster's Biographical Dictionary,*[13] *Merriam Webster's Biographical Dictionary,*[14] *Dictionary of American Biography,*[15] and *Dictionary of National Biography.*[16] For names of living persons, use *Chamber's Biographical Dictionary,*[17] The *Cambridge Biographical Encyclopedia,*[18] and the *Who's Who* series by Marquis; for example, *Who's Who in the World.*[19]

Science-specific biographical dictionaries include such tools as the *Dictionary of Scientific Biography*,[20] which covers deceased scientists, and *Who's Who in Science and Engineering*,[21] which covers over 20,000 current scientific personages worldwide. *American Men and Women of Science*[22] is also a good resource and is available both on-line and in CD-ROM format. As an example of subject-specific scientific biographical information, *American Chemists and Chemical Engineers*[23] provides information about scholars and others in the field. Finally, if a scientist has been written about or has written a book, the Library of Congress Authority File (LCAF) should have information about the correct form of names. This resource can be accessed indirectly through entries in library catalogs or OCLC's FirstSearch Service catalog, WorldCat.[24]

Apart from names of persons, names of organizations can also present trying problems for the indexer. A helpful reference for verification of names of organizations is the *Encyclopedia of Associations: An Associations Unlimited Resource: A Guide to More than 23,000 National and International Organizations*.[25] *Research Centers Directory*[26] covers over 12,800 non-profit U.S. and Canadian research centers, while *European Research Centers*[27] covers Europe. Another resource is *The World of Learning*,[28] which lists the faculty of many universities and other international institutions.

Acronyms

Another indexing problem in science and technology indexing is that of acronyms. In many cases, authors assume that the reader knows the meaning of the acronym, which may not be the case at all. Hence, it is often up to the indexer to verify and provide this information by using dictionaries of acronyms. One of the best general sources is Gale Research's *Acronyms, Initialisms, and Abbreviations Dictionary*[29] and its companions volume, *Reverse Acronyms, Initialisms, and Abbreviations Dictionary: A Companion Volume to Acronyms, Initialisms, and Abbreviations Dictionary with Terms Arranged Alphabetically by Meaning of Acronym, Initialism, or Abbreviation*.[30] Gale also publishes the *International Acronyms, Initialisms, and Abbreviations Dictionary*.[31] U.S. government agencies, notorious for their acronyms, can be determined by the use of the slightly outdated *Guide to Federal Government Acronyms*.[32]

For acronyms specific to science and technology, there is Michael Peschke's International Encyclopedia of Abbreviations and Acronyms in Science and Technology,[33] available in some libraries. Environmental Acronyms, Abbreviations and Glossary of Terms[34] by the EPA (U.S. Environmental Protection

Agency) and the Dictionary of Engineering Acronyms and Abbreviations[35] offer more subject-specific acronym information.

Synonyms and Concepts

Acronyms and names aside, the biggest issue for the science and technology indexer is the inclusion of synonyms and other suitable cross-referencing terms to fully capture the concepts discussed in a text. The nature of scientific research and its broad spectrum demands that indexes be as comprehensive as possible in terms of conceptual terminology. This terminology may not always be referred to by the author, but readers may be looking for it.

Subject-specific reference works thus become extremely important for the indexer when ideas and concepts are not well-defined by the author, when the indexer is not a subject specialist and needs to have help with cross-referencing, or when the book's audience reaches beyond scholars in the discipline. There are literally hundreds of specialized dictionaries, encyclopedias, and thesauri available. Because of space limitations, only a few examples of these types of reference tools are given for several general scientific disciplines. Within each discipline there are different facets so that each has its own reference sources.

Agriculture encompasses a wide range of disciplines, but there are a few general reference tools; for example, the *Dictionary of Agriculture*,[36] which classifies all terms into 81 topics areas in an appendix and provides lists of acronyms, and *The Agriculture Dictionary*.[37]

Up-to-date sources on astronomy are *The Facts on File Dictionary of Astronomy*,[38] which describes over 3,500 terms and concepts in the field, and the *Cambridge Astronomy Dictionary*.[39]

Biology and zoology are represented by *Henderson's Dictionary of Biological Terms*,[40] with over 23,000 entries and acronyms as well, the *Dictionary of Microbiology and Molecular Biology*,[41] which provides synonyms for many entries. Other slightly more up-to-date sources are the *Dictionary of Biochemistry and Molecular Biology*[42] and *The Invertebrates: An Illustrated Glossary*.[43]

Botany is represented by *The Concise Oxford Dictionary of Botany*[44] and the *International Code of Botanical Nomenclature*,[45] which sets the guidelines for naming plants.

Chemistry and physics are also many faceted disciplines and are best represented by the *Handbook of Chemistry and Physics*,[46] a comprehensive source
which contains pages of symbols, terminology, and nomenclature information.
Other helpful resources include *Gardner's Chemical Synonyms and Trade
Names*,[47] *Hawley's Condensed Chemical Dictionary*,[48] and *A Dictionary of
Physics*,[49] which has been revised to include such up-to-date terms as "Higgs
field" and "nanotechnology."

Engineering is broad and wide-ranging field, with nearly a dozen overlapping
subcategories. The *McGraw-Hill Dictionary of Engineering*[50] is an up-to-date
source for general engineering terminology. *INSPEC Thesaurus 1995*[51] and
Ei Thesaurus[52] are also helpful resources for the indexer working in engineering subjects.

Mathematics is covered in part by the famous James *Mathematics Dictionary*,[53]
and *Elsevier's Dictionary of Computer Science and Mathematics: In English,
German, French, and Russian.*[54] Because computer technology is changing so
rapidly, most dictionaries in print in this area are going to have omissions. One
of the more up-to-date print publications in this area is *The Encyclopedia of
Computer Science*,[55] which has been 70% revised with 175 new entries.

How to Find What You Need

If the materials listed here do not answer a specific question that arises,
finding what you need when it comes to a specific indexing problem in a specific subject area is not always easy. K. G. B. Bakewell wrote a helpful article
on basic references for indexers, since revised, which points out general tools
that aid indexers with the indexing process. The materials are arranged by
type of material; i.e., directories, encyclopedias, and the like.[56] However, perhaps the easiest way to find a particular reference book is to ask your local
librarian or look at standard bibliographies of reference books, such as the
American Library Association's latest issue of *Guide to Reference Books*[57] and
*ARBA (American Reference Books Annual) Guide to Subject Encyclopedias
and Dictionaries.*[58] Doing an on-line search of FirstSearch can be fruitful or
fruitless, depending on what terms you use in the search. (See note 24). *Books
in Print*[59] provides information on books currently in print.

Summing Up

Indexers face a number of problems while indexing science and technology
texts. Name verification for persons, organizations, and chemicals are among

these problems, as is extensive use of acronyms. Term selection and cross-referencing of concepts are the most important issues facing the science indexer, who has a wide variety of general and subject-specific reference tools to which to turn. Although the terminology of the author is always the first choice of the indexer, it is usually necessary to create cross-references to and from the author's terms to others that rnight occur to the index user. It behooves the indexer to have a good idea of where those terms are defined, if the author doesn't provide that information.

Notes

[1]William A Katz, *Introduction to Reference Work*, vol.1, 6th ed. (New York: McGraw-Hill. 1992), 24–29.

[2]*Larousse Dictionary of Science and Technology* (New York: Larousse, 1995). ISBN 0752301005 (paperback).

[3]Council of Biology Editors, *Scientific Style and Format: The Manual for Authors, Editors, and Publishers*, 6th ed. (New York: Cambridge, 1994). ISBN 0521471540.

[4]*McGraw-Hill Encyclopedia of Science and Technology*, 8th ed., 20 vols. (New York: McGraw–Hill, 1997). ISBN 0835234630.

[5]Arthur Godman, *The Barnes and Noble Thesaurus of Science: All Fields of Scientific Language Explained and Illustrated* (New York: Barnes and Noble Books, 1983). ISBN 0060151765.

[6]*Thesaurus of Scientific, Technical, and Engineering Terms* (New York: Hemisphere, 1988). ISBN 089116943.

[7]*McGraw-Hill Dictionary of Scientific and Technical Terms* (New York: McGraw-Hill Text, 1994) ISBN 0070423334. (Computer disk also available.)

[8]*Dictionary of Scientific Units: Including Dimensions In Numbers and Scales*, 6th ed. (New York: Chapman and Hall, 1992). ISBN 0412467208.

[9]Cesare Emiliani, *Dictionary of the Physical Sciences: Terms, Formulas, Data* (New York: Oxford University Press, 1987). ISBN 0195036514.

[10]Paul T. Durbin, *Dictionary of Concepts in Philosophy of Science* (New York: Greenwood Publishing Group, 1988). ISBN 0313229791.

[11]Access *Encyclopedia Britannica* through http://www.eb.com. There is a free trial period, and then an inexpensive monthly fee after that.

[12]*Library of Congress Subject Headings*, 19th ed., 4 vols. (Washington, DC: Cataloging Distribution Service, Library of Congress). ISSN 1048–9711.

[13]*Meriam-Webster's New Biographical Dictionary* (Springfield, MA: Merriam Webster, 1995). ISBN 0877797439.

[14]*Webster's Biographical Dictionary* (Springfield, MA: Merriam Webster, 1966).

[15]*Dictionary of American Biography* (New York: Charles Scribner's Sons, 1996). Complete through supplement ten, ISBN 0684804824.

[16]*Dictionary of National Biography*, Sir Leslie Stephen and Sir Sidney Lee, eds. (London: Smith, Elder & Co., 1908–1909, reprint).

[17]*Chamber's Biographical Dictionary*, Rev. ed. (Edinburgh: Chambers, 1990). ISBN 055016040X.

[18]*The Cambridge Biographical Encyclopedia*, Crystal, David, ed. (Cambridge: Cambridge University Press, 1994). ISBN 0521434211.

[19]*Who's Who in the World.* 14th ed. (Wilmette, IL: Marquis Who's Who. 1997). ISBN 0837911176.

[20]Gillispie, Charles Coulston, *Dictionary of Scientific Biography.* 16 vols. (New York: Scribner, 1980). ISBN 0684169622.

[21]*Who's Who in Science and Engineering* (Wilmette, IL: Marquis Who's Who, 1992). ISBN 0837957516.

[22]*American Men and Women of Science, 1995–1996*, 19th ed., 8 vols. (Providence, NJ: R. R. Bowker, 1994). ISBN 0835234630.

[23]*American Chemists and Chemical Engineers.* Vol. 2. Guildford, CT: Gould Books. 1997. ISBN 0964025507.

[24]OCLC is the world's largest bibliographic database and follows Library of Congress and Dewey Decimal classification schemes. FirstSearch WorldCat is the public access version of this database.

[25]*Encyclopedia of Associations: An Associations Unlimited Resource: A Guide to More Than 23,000 National and International Organizations*, 32nd ed. (Detroit, MI: Gale Research, Inc., 1997). ISBN 0787608459.

[26]*Research Centers Directory*, 22nd ed., 2 vols. (Detroit: Gale Research, 1997). ISSN 0080–1518.

[27]*European Research Centers: A Directory of Scientific, Industrial, Agricultural, and Biomedical Laboratories*, 2 vols. (New York: Stockton Press, 1994). ISBN 1561591173.

[28]*The World of Learning, 1997*, 47th ed. (London: Europa Publications, 1997). ISBN 1857430328.

[29]*Acronyms, Initialisms, and Abbreviations Dictionary*, 22nd ed.. (Detroit: Gale Research, 1997). ISBN 0787600369.

[30]*Reverse Acronyms, Initialisms, and Abbreviations Dictionary: A Companion Volume to Acronyms, Initialisms, and Abbreviations Dictionary with Terms Arranged Alphabetically by Meaning of Acronym, Initialism, or Abbreviation*, 22nd ed., 3 vols. (Detroit: Gale Research, 1997).

[31]*International Acronyms, Initialisms, and Abbreviations Dictionary*, 3rd ed. (Detroit: Gale Research, 1993). ISBN 0810374315.

[32]Evinger, William R., ed., *Guide to Federal Government Acronyms*, (Phoenix: Oryx Press, 1989). ISBN 089774586.

[33]Peschke, Michael, *International Encyclopedia of Abbreviations and Acronyms in Science and Technology*, 8 vols. (New Providence, RI: K. G. Saur, 1996). ISBN 3598229704.

[34]*Environmental Acronyms, Abbreviations, and Glossary of Terms*, Environmental Protection Agency (New York: Executive Enterprises Inc., 1994). ISBN 047111250X (paperback).

[35]Keller, Harald and Erb Uwe, *Dictionary of Engineering Acronyms and Abbreviations* (New York: Neal Schuman, 1994). ISBN 1555701299.

[36]Lipton, Kathryn L., *Dictionary of Agriculture* (Boulder, CO: Lynne Rienner Publishing, 1995). ISBN 1555875238.

[37]Herren, Ray V. and Roy L. Donahue, *The Agriculture Dictionary* (Albany, NY: Delmar Publishers, 1991). ISBN 0827340974 (paperback).

[38]llingworth, Valerie, ed., *The Facts on File Dictionary of Astronomy* (New York: Facts on File, 1995). ISBN 016031851.

[39]Ridpath, Ian, ed., *Cambridge Astronomy Dictionary* (New York: Cambridge University Press, 1996). ISBN 0521589916.

[40]Lawrence, Eleanor, *Henderson's Dictionary of Biological Terms*, 11th ed. (New York: John Wiley & Sons, 1995). ISBN 0470235071.

[41]Singleton, Paul and Diana Sainsbury, *Dictionary of Microbiology and Molecular Biology*, 2nd ed. (New York: John Wiley & Sons, 1987). ISBN 0471940526 (paperback).

[42]Stenesh, Jochanan, *Dictionary of Biochemistry and Molecular Biology* (New York: John Wiley & Sons, 1989). ISBN 0471840890.

[43]Stachowitsch, Michael, *The Invertebrates: An Illusrated Glossary* (New York: Wiley–Liss, 1992). ISBN 0471561924 (paperback).

[44]Allaby, Michael, ed., *The Concise Oxford Dictionary of Botany* (New York: Oxford, 1992). ISBN 0192860941.

[45]Greuther, W., *International Code of Botanical Nomenclature* (Champaign, IL: Koeltz Science Books, 1988). ISBN 3874292789.

[46]*Handbook of Chemistry and Physics: A Ready Reference Book of Chemical and Physical Data* (Boca Raton: CRC Press, annual).

[47]Ash, Michael and Irene, *Gardner's Chemical Synonyms and Trade Names* (Brookfield, VT: Ashgate Publishing Co., 1994). ISBN 0566074915.

[48]*Hawley's Condensed Chemical Dictionary*, 13th ed. (New York: Van Nostrand Reinhold, 1997). ISBN 0442023243. (To be released August 1997).

[49]lsaacs, Alan, ed., *A Dictionary of Physics* (New York: Oxford, 1996). ISBN 0192800302.

[50]*McGraw-Hlll Dictionary of Engineering,* (New York: McGraw-Hill, 1997). ISBN 0070524351.

[51]*INSPEC Thesaurus, 1995,* (London: Institution of Electrical Engineers, 1995). ISBN 0852969643.

[52]*Thesaurus*, Rev. 2nd ed. (Hoboken, NJ: Engineering Information, Inc., 1995). 1SBN 0873941446.

[53]James, Robert C., *Mathematics Dictionary*, 5th ed. (New York: Chapman and Hall, 1992). ISBN 0442007418 (paperback).

[54]Deliiska, Boriana, *Elsevier's Dictionary of Computer Science and Mathematics: In English, German, French, and Russian* (New York: Elsevier Science, 1995). ISBN 0444818162.

[55]Ralston, R., *The Encyclopedia of Computer Science* (New York: Van Nostrand Reinhold, 1997).

[56]Bakewell, K. G. B., "Reference books for indexers." *The Indexer* 15 (1987):131–40, 195–96. This has been updated as a publication of the Society of Indexers as *Infor-*

mation Sources and Reference Tools, by K. G. B. Bakewell, 2nd ed. Revised by Pat. F. Booth, 1993. ISBN 1871577101.

[57]*Guide to Reference Books,* 11th ed. (Chicago: American Library Association, 1996). ISBN 0838906699.

[58]*ARBA Guide to Subject Encyclopedias and Dictionaries,* 2nd ed. (Englewood, CO: Libraries Unlimited, 1997). ISBN 1563084678.

[59]*Books in Print* (R. R. Bowker: New York, annual).

Index